Hannes Androsch

Afloat on a Turbulent Ocean

A Reflective View of Austria in the 20th Century

Hannes Androsch

Afloat on a Turbulent Ocean

A Reflective View of Austria in the 20th Century

Für
Barbara Prammer
in freundschaftlicher
Verbundenheit und
mit herzlichen Wünschen
Hannes Androsch
Wien, 26.06.07

StudienVerlag
Innsbruck, Wien, Bozen

 | **Corporate design** by Kurt Höretzeder | **Layout:** Studienverlag/Karin Berner | This book is printed on acid-free paper. | **Bibliographic information published by Die Deutsche Bibliothek:** Die Deutsche Bibliothek lists this publication in the Deutsche Nationalbibliographie; detailed bibliographic data is available on the Internet at http://dnb.ddb.de | Distributed in North America and South America and the rest of the world excluding Austria, Germany, and Switzerland by: Transaction Publishers, Rutgers – The State University, 35 Berrue Circle, Piscataway New Jersey, 08854-8042, USA, www.transactionpub.com.
Based on the book in German "Economy and Society. Austria 1945–2005" (Vienna Lectures – Dialogue Forum of the City of Vienna: series "Austria – The Second Republic: Findings, Review, and Prospects", edited by Hubert Christian Ehalt on behalf of the Cultural Division of the City of Vienna, in total 20 volumes)
ISBN 978-3-7065-4494-8

Afloat on a Turbulent Ocean

Table of Contents

Preface

Anniversaries are not just a cause for celebration, but rather an occasion and an impulse to reflect. Some of these reflections can dwell on matters that touch our very essence, evocative thoughts about our history and our identity.

And so it came to pass in Austria in the year 2005. We celebrated, we honoured and we criticised. We staged exhibitions, held guest lectures and wrote books. The idea for this book germinated amid all this activity when I was invited to provide a manuscript on the history of the Second Republic, with the title "*Economy and Society. Austria 1945–2005*", for the Vienna Lectures series. This appeared in the series "*Austria – The Second Republic: Findings, Review and Prospects*".

Two years later, as the edition was almost sold out, the suggestion arose to update and revise the edition; at the same time, it was decided to produce an English language, hence international, edition as well. Added impetus was given by the realisation that the year 2007 provided yet more reasons to celebrate; this year is the 50th anniversary of the signing of the Treaties of Rome and the 60th anniversary of the announcement of the Truman doctrine on which the Marshall Plan was based. These were important landmarks in the creation and promotion of European integration, an idea inspired by Jean Monnet and made reality by the creation of the European Coal and Steel Community (known as the ECSC or *Montanunion*). That this anniversary and the associated celebrations should generate less public enthusiasm than some national or Austrian anniversaries, serves to show that even after 50 years, there is very little to see of a European-based "patriotism".

It is precisely this antiquated, Austro-centric attitude which I try to avoid in this publication through a suitable choice of viewpoints and issues. I try to find a way to integrate recent Austrian history into its proper global context. I am convinced that it is no longer possible to appreciate the history of any country without looking beyond the national borders of the country in question. Nor can one report on recent events which shape the world in which we live without training our focus on their implications for the future. Consequently, I seek to weave an informal and coherent literary tapestry which interlinks Austrian developments of the 20th century, Europe of the present and global perspectives of the future.

This book is consciously written for an international audience, and it deals substantially with the development of a global society, within which Austria can be viewed as a central European component, or case study. For, even if our small nation will appear as a dot, at most, when depicted on a map of the World, as Austrians, we nevertheless have a valid viewpoint to express. Thus, this book makes no great claim to scientific objectivity, nor is it the work of a historian; rather, it should be viewed as an essay which treats history from the perspective of a "journalist looking backwards", to borrow an expression from the celebrated Austrian writer, Karl Kraus. As such, it reflects in certain episodes the subjective views and observations of the author. When one writes about a period in history which one not only experienced, but influenced to a certain degree, a measure of subjectivity cannot be avoided.

I wish to express my sincere thanks to various colleagues who were actively involved in producing this book, for their valuable and tireless assistance in discussing ideas and in reading the manuscript. In addition, I owe a special debt of gratitude to Jessica Jarosch and Renate Platzer for their research and editing skills, and above all to Ciarán Cassidy and Gunhild Kiesenhofer-Widhalm for their many English language suggestions and advice.

Hannes Androsch
Vienna, May 2007

A Year of Anniversaries

The year 2005 presents an exceptional confluence of anniversaries and commemorative events, which Austria needs to celebrate in a spirit of festivity but also to contemplate in a spirit of critical self-appraisal. Sixty years ago we experienced liberation from warfare and Nazi domination. It is fifty years since we regained our freedom with the signing of the "*Staatsvertrag*", or State Treaty, which signalled the withdrawal of the Allied forces of post-war occupation.

We also commemorate events which are part and parcel of the restoration of independent statehood in Austria: Our armed forces were re-established fifty years ago; Austria has also been a member of the United Nations for the same length of time, and the reopening of the Burgtheater and Staatsoper, leading institutions of their kind in the world and indispensable to our image as a "cultural" nation, also took place exactly half a century ago. Somewhat less home-grown, but nevertheless worthy of celebration, is the tenth anniversary of Austria's membership of the European Union. Our country's accession to the Union was preceded by a referendum, in which our population ratified the decision to accede by an overwhelming majority. Five years ago, the euro was introduced by twelve EU member states as their common currency and since 2002 it has been in circulation as our sole medium of exchange.

Our list of anniversaries, to celebrate and contemplate, is by no means at an end. This year, Austria commemorates the 85th anniversary of its first constitution, 50 years of television, and the centenary of the award of the Nobel Peace Prize to Bertha von Suttner. Von Suttner, who is also commemorated on the Austrian two euro coin, was the leading pacifist and activist in the thirty years prior to World War I, and wrote the seminal anti-war book "Lay Down Your Arms" (*Die Waffen nieder!*).

Some other events are no less worthy of commemoration even if they do not inspire public awareness to quite the same extent. Foremost among those is the General Social Insurance Act (*Allgemeines Sozialversicherungsgesetz, or ASVG*), which became law fifty years ago and which is a corner stone of our welfare state. At that time, social expenditure amounted to 15% of our GDP, whereas today, this ratio has climbed to almost 30%. It should therefore come as no surprise that taxation as a proportion of GDP has also risen from about 28.8 % to 42.2 % over the same time period.

This year also marks the thirtieth anniversary of the final declaration of the CSCE-conference in Helsinki on 1 August 1975. This declaration provided the moral justification and political motivation for downtrodden and oppressed people in centrally-planned economies to agitate for their freedom and for human rights. The importance of this final declaration in the collapse of the Soviet Empire has been greatly underestimated. The fact is that it was an important catalyst which served to expose the internal contradictions of the Soviet system and, thus, contributed handsomely to overcoming the deep divisions within Europe.

The *Creditanstalt* bank, once the star of our financial system and the number one calling card for our country internationally, would also have celebrated 150 years of existence this year had it not been allowed, quite unnecessarily, to disappear from the financial firmament.

And, thirty-five years ago this year heralded the beginning of the "Kreisky Era", which contributed so significantly to the modernisation and economic success of our country during the Second Republic. This thirty-year era, which amounts to one half of the sixty years which have elapsed since the end of World War II in 1945, is significant for the fact that the Social Democratic Party (SPÖ) continuously filled the office of the chancellor. In this context we can also commemorate the 40th anniversary of the death of Adolf Schärf, who served his country for so long and is chiefly remembered as a founder member of the Social Democratic Party, co-negotiator of the State Treaty and, last but not least, as President of Austria.

No Future without Remembrance

Other anniversaries occurring in 2005 bring forth much sadder memories. It is sixty years since the survivors of the holocaust were freed from their torment in the Nazi concentration camps of Auschwitz, Mauthausen and many other centres of suffering. It is ten years since the Roma population in Oberwart, Austria was submitted to the racist atrocity of booby-trap bombs. We cannot afford to forget those events: In this spirit, let us recall the famous *dictum* attributed to Primo Levi; "He who does not remember, has no future".

If we take a broader historical perspective, other important anniversaries come into focus. Following the battle of the three emperors near *Austerlitz* two hundred years ago, the Archbishopric of Salzburg came into the possession of Austria. And, arguably, even more significant is the five-hundred-year jubilee of the lands around *Rattenberg, Kitzbühel* and *Kufstein*, in addition to parts of the *Salzkammergut*, encompassing the lakes *Mondsee* and *Wolfgangsee*, passing into the possession of the Habsburgs, thus becoming part of Austria.

Looking beyond the borders of Austria, one cannot overlook other landmark anniversaries. The year 2005 also marks the 250th anniversary of the death of the French legal expert Montesquieu (1689–1755), or to give him his full name and title, Charles-Louis de Secondat Baron de la Brède et de Montesquieu. This enlightened political philosopher first expounded his doctrine of the separation of powers in 1748, which thus entitles him to recognition as the founding father of the modern constitutional state.

Three hundred years ago, in 1705, Bernard de Mandeville first published his landmark poem, "*Grumbling Hive*", which he later revised and re-published as "*The Fable of the Bees*" and which bore the enigmatic subtitle "private vice, public virtue". Although this satirical poem earned de Mandeville, a Dutch doctor living in Britain, notoriety and public abuse, it has proven to exert a lasting influence on all the great economic philosophers since Adam Smith and David Hume, including Immanuel Kant and Karl Marx. One could even argue that it also anticipated John

Maynard Keynes's "Paradox of Thrift" which many would regard as a key economic insight of the 20th century. Keynes can be seen to have inverted de Mandeville's celebrated slogan, as Keynes's "paradox" can be summarised as "private virtue, public vice".

In his poem, de Mandeville described how perceived personal vices, such as avarice, the quest for luxury, greed, envy and vanity, were, in reality, social virtues which ensured the greatest good of society. Their exercise led directly to the employment of millions of the poor who would otherwise starve. This pursuit of personal "self interest", as these private vices were later categorised, was essential for the welfare of the nation as a whole. Thus, de Mandeville is seen to provide the intellectual basis, and justification, for the free-enterprise market economy.

Although the value of de Mandeville's insight is widely recognised today, no one subscribes to it completely and without reservation. Lord Edward Heath, a former Conservative Prime Minister of the United Kingdom, once described the predatory activities of multi-national companies in the Third World as "the unacceptable face of capitalism". Unrestrained self interest is no longer seen as the fundamental principle of social organisation, as depicted in de Mandeville's beehive, because the principle of equality, in particular equality of opportunity, and the indispensability of social justice for political cohesion and economic prosperity, serve to restrict its worst excesses.

International literature has also many occasions to celebrate in 2005. First, we have the "Schiller Year" as 2005 marks the bicentenary of the death of the poet. It is also the "Stifter Year" as the writer Adalbert Stifter was born two hundred years ago, as were Hans Christian Andersen and Elias Canetti. This year also marks the 25th anniversary of the death of Jean Paul Sartre who, incidentally, was born one hundred years ago.

Film fans will know that 2005 is also the 50th anniversary of the untimely and accidental death of the iconic actor, James Dean. His portrayal of the alienation and rebelliousness of adolescence became the hallmark, and to some the inspiration, of an era.

However, neither joyful nor reflective commemorative occasions should give rise to a sense of smug self-satisfaction or to an exaggerated feeling of conceit, arrogance or self-importance. Instead, the opportunity should be taken to examine critically the role our past has played in shaping our present, and to expose our innermost values and attitudes to the spotlight of critical self-appraisal. In this sense, we can only agree with Trautl Brandstaller, the recognised intellectual and social commentator, who posed the warning question, if it might not be more appropriate to take the year 2004 as our focal point for identifying important anniversaries? After all, some important dates which correlate with 2004 conjure up events which are less celebratory, and which pose some searching questions concerning Austria's recent history.

Three such dates spring readily to mind; 28 July 1914, 12 February 1934 and 20 July 1944. Each of these dates represents a watershed in our recent history. The first marked the opening shots of the First World War, in which we were involved as the Austro-Hungarian Empire, and which would prove to be the beginning of the end of the monarchy. The second date represents the beginning of the civil war in Austria, which culminated in the Austro-fascist constitution and heralded the end of democracy in the First Republic. Finally, the third date was the day on which the Stauffenberg assassination attempt on Adolf Hitler, organised in the hope of bringing the national-socialist dictatorship to an early end, failed in its objective. The consequence of this failure would be the deaths of many more millions of people.

We live in an age of abbreviations, of symbols, where major events are often reduced in the public awareness to a gesture, a picture or a sound bite. These are all over-simplifications of sometimes quite complex and protracted events; while this helps us to construct mental catalogues of astounding amounts of information, it can rarely do justice to the events themselves.

In this way, history is reduced to a series of anniversaries and key dates, and historical events are abbreviated to a few widely-recognised symbolic gestures or pronouncements. Thus, we remember Leopold Figl, the first post-war chancellor of Austria, and recall his legendary address to the nation at Christmas 1945 primarily because of the appeal to his listeners, "*Glaubt an dieses Österreich*" ("Believe in this Austria"); or, the well-known photo-image "four in a jeep" which, for many, encapsulates ten years of occupation by the four allied powers following the Second World War. Arguably, best known of all is the oft-repeated image of Leopold Figl, standing on the balcony of the Belvedere Palace on 15 May 1955, showing the newly signed State Treaty to the assembled multitude, and uttering the immortal words, "*Österreich ist frei!*" ("Austria is free!").

Because these images have been repeated so often in the media, they have come to symbolise the birth of the Second Republic in our collective awareness. Yet, for individuals who lived through this period, or who may have contributed in some way to the events as they unfolded, personal recollections will also play an important part in their perception of this momentous historical occasion.

Just as the history of the Second Republic cannot be captured by a single date – not even the Republic's moment of birth on 27 April 1945 – neither can it be tied to a single location. None of the prominent associations, the Town Hall of Vienna, the Upper Belvedere, Vienna itself, can capture the complexity of historical events. If history can be compared to a tapestry of inter-woven events, then a proper understanding of history requires an equally sophisticated intellectual process.

Men of the Century: Einstein and Gandhi

Albert Einstein died fifty years ago. One hundred years ago, his Theory of Relativity turned the scientific community's perception of the world upside down. Time magazine proclaimed Einstein, just ahead of Gandhi, as the "man of the century". In many ways, these two symbolise the history of the 20th century.

Einstein himself, in conjunction with his Theory of Relativity, stands as a symbol for revolutionary scientific discoveries, technological change, technical progress, and all the repercussions and consequences of these phenomena. Scientific research into the macro-cosmos as well as the micro-cosmos has progressed rapidly in our time and greatly enhanced our understanding of the working of the universe.

Many developments and discoveries have influenced our lives to an extent we could scarcely even imagine beforehand. Amongst these we would have to include electricity, oil, mechanisation, atomic energy, aeronautics, telecommunications (and in particular, mobile telecommunications), space exploration, new materials, new production techniques, the widespread use of computers, the internet, radio and especially television, the mechanisation of agriculture and with it the explosive growth in food production and, last but not least, the mechanisation of private households.

In 1945, the world still experienced acute shortages which were most noticeable in the areas of foodstuffs, energy products, vehicles, building materials, and much more. Soon we were to witness waves of new fashions, or fads, in eating habits, dress styles, furnishing, motorisation and holidays. In the meantime we have developed into a society with an egoistic obsession with leisure-time activities and hedonistic pleasure seeking. In Austria, the working week has been shortened from 48 hours to 38; minimum annual holidays have grown from two weeks to five. This pronounced shift in favour of leisure associated with the reduction in working hours has been a consistent feature of all western economies.

In the 20th century, we live in the era of sports, by now an indispensable part of our leisure culture. Sad to say, our sporting activity is all too often experienced in a purely passive manner in front of the ubiquitous television set, giving rise to the unflattering expression “the couch potato”.

Fifty years ago we had 150,000 motor cars in Austria; today the number is 4.2 million and growing rapidly. Fifty years ago we had 507,149 telephone lines, of which 106,405 were only quarter, i.e. shared, lines; today we have over 6 million mobile telephone subscribers. This astonishing increase in mobility, along with the expansion in communications networks, has completely transformed our understanding and perception of the world.

Einstein's biography is itself a reflection of the 20th century. It represents the persecution and expulsion of Europe's elites, the tidal "brain drain" which was driven by the racial madness of the demonic Nazi regime. This culminated in the apocalypse of the holocaust. Sixty years on, we can take the anniversary of the liberation as a special opportunity to reflect on this gruesome spectre – and resolve, never to forget! Quite recently, the assembly of nations under the auspices of the United Nations held a commemorative ceremony for those who died in the death camp of Auschwitz; the anniversary of the liberation of the survivors of the concentration camp is 27 January.

Remembrance of such events makes us aware that we carry a very special responsibility. Specifically, we must be vigilant that crimes against humanity, which can be symbolically represented by "Auschwitz", must never be allowed to happen again.

To keep this memory alive, we must remind ourselves continuously of the crimes against humanity perpetrated in the name of national-socialism, to anchor these facts in our consciousness and never let them go. Prior to 1938, some 185,000 Jews lived in Vienna; today no more than a tiny fraction of these remain. The Jewish religious community has a membership of about 6,000. We know that 65,000 Austrian Jews were murdered in the Nazi concentration camps and that the vast majority of the survivors of the Holocaust never returned to Austria – a monumental human, intellectual and cultural blood-letting. An important part of our year of commemoration must be an expression of reverence for the survivors, as well as one of mourning the deceased victims of the Mauthausen concentration camp, whose liberation took place on 15 May 1945.

Gandhi is no less significant than Einstein as a symbolic icon of the 20th century and he, too, stands for dramatic upheaval. His policy of passive resistance became an irresistible weapon of liberation in the hands of down – trodden people everywhere and signalled the end of the colonial domination by the European superpowers.

The colonial empires, and above all the British Empire, disintegrated in the aftermath of the Second World

War. The loss of India, Pakistan and other Asian colonies meant an end to the exploitation of the resources of those territories, and thus undermined the economic viability of the Empire. Consequential and unavoidable cost-cutting led to "voluntary" withdrawal from other regions, such as the Middle East, although Gibraltar and the Falklands show us, each in their own way, that empires rarely surrender so much as a clump of rock entirely voluntarily. The tragedy of the Middle East, including the injustices still inflicted on many peoples living there, is still very much with us and can be dated to British involvement and the Balfour Declaration. There is no such thing as a benevolent empire, and the evil it perpetrates frequently outlives it.

The importance of Gandhi's mass movement of passive resistance goes far beyond the liberation of the Indian sub-continent from British colonial rule. The political and social domination of one group by another is best combated with passive resistance, be it colonialism, apartheid, racism, bigotry, gerrymandering or any other form of inequality and oppression. Gandhi was the inspiration for the civil rights movement in the United States as well as the anti-apartheid movement in South Africa and elsewhere. His message was, and is, that superiority of arms may suffice to conquer a people, but is not enough to keep them in thrall. The advent of global news coverage, especially via television, has magnified the efficacy of passive resistance as a "weapon against oppression" beyond all imagination.

The demise of the European empires has provided the opportunity for several of the "ancient countries", with their ancient cultures and massive populations, to return to the centre stage of world events. China, India and Brazil are primary examples of this new trend.

The Age of Extremes

Eric Hobsbawm, the historian and social scientist, once described the 20th century as the *short century* in his renowned book, *The Age of Extremes*. What he meant was that the 20th century, as an epoch, lasted to all intents and purposes from the beginning of the First World War to the end of the Cold War. As extremes, he contrasted the unprecedented economic prosperity and greater personal freedom on the one hand, with the Holocaust and the Stalinist Gulag-system on the other. The period up to 1945 was particularly "bloody" and characterised Europe as the "dark continent" (Mark Mazower), in which Europe's global importance diminished rapidly.

Catastrophes and change also tend to be accompanied and marked by social transition and this period was no exception. The status of women and of youth changed dramatically, as did family structures and the population pyramid. As if adversity had made us pliant, society discovered a new tolerance towards non-conformist behaviour – highlighted in the de-criminalisation of the gay community, understanding towards those who drop out of the "rat race", acceptance of the moral validity of conscientious objection to war and participation in the military – as well as a more open and caring towards sufferers of mental and physical disabilities and other forms of personal misfortune.

The character of democracy also deepened as the population became more confident in thinking for itself, and no longer accepted unquestioningly the views of governments or ruling elites. Growing environmental awareness, not to mention the emergence of the Green Movement as a political force, is a product of the past few decades and the unsustainable lifestyle we have rushed to create for ourselves. Against this changing backdrop, a variety of so called NGOs, or non-government organisations, have acquired growing social and political significance.

Meanwhile, the Cold War came to an end in an epoch-ending flash, the *annus mirabilis* 1989. This time of dramatic upheaval, cataclysmic change and destabilising turmoil now lies decidedly behind us. It is being followed by a period of accelerating change as two dramatic events which followed each other in rapid succession, can serve to illustrate. The first was the fall of the Berlin Wall on 9 November 1989, which symbolically ended the hegemony of the Soviet system in Central Europe and facilitated the reunification of Germany. The second occurred in New York on

11 September 2001 as two hijacked airliners were flown into the twin towers of the World Trade Centre.

In the midst of accelerated change, dramatic events and joyous causes of celebration, and in the midst of historical evolution where nothing makes much sense without an understanding of what went before, it is appropriate to ask ourselves how we would assess Austria's current position in this densely-woven tapestry that is history.

In contrast to the First Republic which no one really wanted, the Second Republic presents a never-ending success story of which we may justifiably be proud. If today we rank the industrial nations of the world in terms of their *per capita* income, we see that Austria occupies the 6th position. It was, indeed, a precarious path from the hardship of a fragmented and polarised First Republic, in whose survival or welfare few would have placed much hope, to the much more satisfactory and acceptable circumstances of the present.

The First Republic: A State No One Wanted

The republic which was proclaimed on 12 November 1918 was little more than an object retrieved from the pawned, bankrupt mass of the empire of nations at the end of the war; an artificial creation of the victor nations, a state condemned to everlasting diminutive status. As Norbert Leser, the Austrian political and social philosopher, has shown, its people suffered from "reduction shock". This Austria was a state created without consensus, a "state which no one wanted" (Hellmut Andics), an "unloved state" (Friedrich Weissensteiner).

To many, the diminutive state of Austria which emerged from the Conference of Versailles and the Treaty of Saint-Germain was a classic example of an imposed solution, constructed by war victors who had little understanding for what they were doing, or for the long-term implications of their decisions. As a future blueprint for Europe, it proved to be disastrous, and was a reason why so many rejected it as a concept and were prepared to see their future in a Pan-German state. Unfortunately, this aspiration was spearheaded by the German Nazi party, and Adolf Hitler.

Scarcely another country was as adversely affected by the consequences of the First World War as Austria. Because of its lack of internal cohesion, the country was quite incapable of withstanding the structural changes and shifts that affected it, the unfavourable international environment and, finally, the repercussions of worldwide recession. This can be seen from the failure of banks and stock exchanges as well as the collapse of insurance companies and other financial institutions.

However, the country would have been more than viable had the available resources been utilised efficiently. The First Republic was better positioned than many other countries, and wealthier than it believed itself to be. Iron ore, mineral oil and water power were available, even if unexploited and underutilised. The country still possessed an extensive industrial infrastructure and, above all, there was an impressive potential of creative and inventive people available. The wounds of the First World War were by no means as deep as those following the Second World War, although the deprivation suffered by the population was greater. Thus, there is really no reason to believe that the First Republic was inevitably doomed to failure. The demise of the First Republic cannot be blamed on a lack of opportunity, but rather on a lack of faith, and confidence in the country's ability to survive. An important role was also played by the increasingly unfavourable external environment, as the renowned journalist, Hugo Portisch, indicated in his path-breaking historical documentary, *Österreich I.*

The young republic suffered from a devastating hyperinflation, struggled under the crushing burden of mass unemployment and despaired at the crippling level of foreign debt. The world economic crisis of 1929 caught Austria with particular force, exacerbated by the fact that the country was in a long-term recession. The country's gross national product had not yet regained the level it had attained in 1913, and would not reach again until the middle of the 20th century. A further surge in the army of the unemployed was the consequence. How distressing this was for the afflicted can scarcely be imagined today. In Austria, the complete loss of hope, the despair, which affected so many was dramatically highlighted by the pioneering sociological study by Paul Lazarsfeld and Maria Jahoda, "*Die Arbeitslosen von Marienthal*" (The Unemployed in Marienthal). This justly-famous study was one of the very first sociological field-studies of its kind in the world.

Poverty and Economic Destitution

Budgetary passivity, or procrastination, was a common form of fiscal inactivity in all countries in the 1930s. Typically, governments sat back and waited for the recovery phase of the business cycle to "correct" cyclically-induced budgetary deficits. The ideology of non-intervention in the economy was widely regarded as correct, and was even supported by the legendary Austrian economist, Friedrich Hayek; the role of government in steering and managing the economy was not then understood as it is today. Tragically, this can be viewed as a contributory factor to the intensity and persistence of the worldwide recession which followed the Wall Street crash of 1929.

It would take another decade before unemployment came to be regarded as a specific responsibility of government. All this changed after 1936 with the publication of John Maynard Keynes's path-breaking book, the "*General Theory of Employment, Interest and Money*". The key insight of this book was that there was no market-based mechanism in the economy which would automatically counteract demand-deficient unemployment. Consequently, the key recommendation of this book, the advocacy of deficit spending on public-works programmes to alleviate unemployment in recession, changed the nature of government economic policy fundamentally and permanently.

But while Keynes provided the theoretical justification, he was by no means the first to advocate this policy solution. Before him, Hjalmar Schacht, who as president of the *Reichsbank* (the German central bank) had helped bring the post-war German hyperinflation under control and who served as economics minister in Germany from 1934–1937, had already used public-works programmes extensively to ameliorate the consequences of unemployment. The construction of the German *Autobahn*, or highways, was the outstanding example of his efforts. At the same time, Franklin D. Roosevelt implemented a wide range of programmes under the umbrella of his "New Deal" in the USA. Many of these faced considerable opposition, but the Tennessee Valley Authority, the Securities and Exchange Commission (SEC), and social security are lasting monuments to his policy, and memory.

Austrian attempts to overcome the widespread economic suffering of the Great Depression remained by and large unsuccessful. Abandoned by the international community, Austria came more and more under the economic influence of Italy, and especially, Germany. It was an age when adversity led to a fundamental questioning of the efficacy of the capitalist system in many countries, and led some to advocate the superiority of an alternative, be it the communist or the fascist political-economic systems. The apparent success of the "economic miracle" in Germany created a gloss for the fascist system which many, unaware of the reality beneath the gloss, found particularly attractive.

The post WW I atmosphere of despair led to an intensification of political tensions in the country. It was not until the Second Republic that the dominant influence of conservative Catholicism in political life waned, largely thanks to the moderating influence of Cardinal Franz König, Archbishop of Vienna. By coincidence, our jubilee year 2005 is also the centenary of his birth.

However, in the 1920s, various factions on the right and on the left of the political spectrum began to form paramilitary groupings. In a climate of growing anarchy, clashes between these groups were inevitable. In January 1927, a right-wing group in *Schattendorf, Burgenland,* fired upon a left-wing socialist-republican demonstration, killing some participants. The subsequent acquittal of the assailants kindled emotions to such a pitch that a workers' group stormed and burned the *Justizpalast*, or Palace of Justice, which housed the court. In the fighting, 84 civilians and 4 policemen on sentry duty were killed and over 1,000 people wounded.

Amid the growing anarchy, Engelbert Dollfuß was appointed chancellor and foreign minister in 1932, a position he held until his assassination during an attempted coup by members of the Austrian Nazi party on 25 July 1934. His short two years in power have remained a matter of heated controversy ever since. On 4 March 1933, and on the basis of a wartime special-powers act which had never been revoked, Dollfuß abolished parliament, introduced press censorship and banned all public meetings and demonstrations to be held by the socialists, the communists or the national socialists. Some argue that this measure was undertaken to thwart a possible electoral victory of the Nazis, who were gaining in popularity.

Thereafter, Dollfuß assumed dictatorial powers and ruled by decree. The corporatist state he created under the influence of Mussolini, and which lasted until the German Nazi invasion in 1938, is commonly described as the period of Austro-Fascism. An attempt to disarm the socialists in February 1934 led to a brief, if intense, civil war which claimed almost 1,600 casualties, both dead and wounded. Then, in July 1934, an abortive coup, the *Juliputsch,* by the Austrian Nazi party claimed several victims, but prominent among them was the chancellor, who was shot in his office. This single and final event in his life had the effect, in the eyes of many, of transforming the perpetrator of fascism into its most celebrated victim.

The deflationary economic policies of Austro-Fascism created a strong national currency and a very high level of foreign exchange reserves. However, they had disastrous consequences for the almost 600,000 unemployed in the country, about 40% of whom did not qualify for any form of public assistance.

But worse was to come in the form of the tyranny and the lunacy of the Nazi regime. The jubilation witnessed when the German troops invaded Austria in March 1938, and again at the Nazi parade on *Heldenplatz* in Vienna a few days later, cannot be understood or explained without an extensive grasp of background events. In this context we need to express our gratitude to Manfred Scheuch, historian and newspaper editor, whose book *Der Weg zum Heldenplatz* (The Road to Heldenplatz) first provided a summary of Austrian dictatorship and traced this period of Austrian history. Incidentally, the recent book by Günther Steinbach, *Kanzler, Krisen, Katastrophen* (Chancellors, Crises and Catastrophes) is an extremely readable, accessible and comprehensive account of the history of the First Republic.

Within days of the German occupation of Austria, the bumper reserves of the Austrian central bank were transferred by the Nazis to Berlin – amounting to 78.3 tonnes of fine gold and 60.2 million schillings in foreign exchange reserves. The German *Reichsbank*, effectively bankrupt from the policies of the Nazi party, was thus kept liquid for a further nine months of wartime preparation. Back in Austria, charitable organisations, including the Bavarian food-train, were distributing food packages amongst the population.

A Brown Requiem

Forced emigration, victims of war both at home and as part of the resistance, poverty and distress, suffering, agony and destruction, these were the consequences of the Nazi dictatorship. Many Austrians were tacit supporters of the German invasion and the renowned actors Helmut Qualtinger and Karl Merz have portrayed their personality in the stage character they created, the "Herr Karl". Regrettably, more than a few were also active supporters.

The *Anschluss*, or the amalgamation of German and Austria, held a considerable attraction for many Austrians especially before it became a reality. To them, and their number included many socialists, the "*Großdeutsche Lösung*" or integration of Austria into the *Weimarer Republik*, offered the best prospect of escape from economic adversity. It was only after March 1938 that the horror of this option became apparent to all. The disillusionment of the socialist movement following the annexation was graphically described in his memoirs by Adolf Schärf, who subsequently served as president of Austria.

It will always remain a rather depressing thought that a significant part of the Austrian population openly expressed their jubilation at the military conquest of our country by the German forces on 13 March 1938. This seemingly inexplicable response only begins to make sense when it is viewed against the circumstances and turbulence of the previous decade – economic destitution, internal social fragmentation, polarisation of political views and, last but not least, the persecution of dissenters by the Austro-fascist dictatorship, precipitated by the disasters of 1933 and 1934. Otherwise, it is not possible to make sense of the response. These political developments reached their ignoble and nightmarish nadir in the events of 15 March on *Heldenplatz* (Heroes Square) in Vienna as the country careered out of control into the abyss.

Nevertheless, it is completely false to contend that the *Anschluss*, or annexation of Austria, was welcomed by all Austrians as "the fulfilment of a historical and legal destiny". The jubilant crowd on *Heldenplatz*, exaggerated as Hugo Portisch has shown it to be by Nazi propaganda film-makers, must be contrasted with the far-greater number of those who stayed away and who sat at home, fearful and full of foreboding. Let us recall that active resistance emerged in the immediate aftermath of the invasion which also claimed its victims. To those we owe our deepest respect.

From the very first moment, the Nazis set off in relentless pursuit of their opponents. In the short period of about four weeks between the German invasion and the pseudo plebiscite staged by Hitler, the Gestapo made about 76,000 arrests. On 1 April 1938, about ten days before the plebiscite, the first political detainees were brought to Dachau. Among them were many who later became leading political figures of the Second Republic: Fritz Bock, Robert Danneberg, Leopold Figl, Alfons Gorbach, Franz Olah, Karl Seitz, Otto Probst, Rosa Jochmann and many more suddenly found themselves in the alleyways of the concentration camps.

But the sheer horror of the holocaust exceeds anything we can conceivably comprehend today. The death toll of the warring nations during the Second World War, which is widely estimated to have cost over 60 million lives, cannot really be compared to the wilful murder of more than 6 million Jews, and well over 12 million when we consider the similar fate of other "undesirable" minorities. This destruction of human life must be seen as the hallmark of the racist ideology of national-socialism. A clear and premeditated intent to murder on the part of the national-socialist dictatorship underpinned this policy of brutal extermination. This organisation of mass murder as an industrial process must surely rank as one of the most shocking innovations in all of European history.

While one may express shock at the indifference of many Austrians to the fate of their Jewish fellow citizens, other European countries hardly distinguished themselves in their efforts to make good this deficiency. Without question, had other countries shown more generosity of spirit and a greater willingness to help in 1938 and 1939, tens of thousands of lives could have been saved. Austria has learned from this episode. Since 1945, it has become one of the foremost destinations for asylum seekers in Europe. Since 1945, almost two million people have found freedom, either in Austria, or using Austria as a transit land. Among them were 500,000 Jews – 400,000 in the 1970s alone – who came mainly from the Soviet Union and other countries of Eastern Europe.

During the Hungarian uprising in 1956, some 256,000 Hungarians fled to Austria; following the events of 1968, some 100,000 Czechs and Slovaks, and in the period following 1979 some 60,000 Poles found refuge in Austria. As a consequence of martial law, which was proclaimed in Poland in 1980/81, some 150,000 Polish citizens stayed in Austria, at least temporarily. During the war in the Balkans in the 1990s, Austria offered asylum to some 80,000 refugees from Bosnia.

The Brown Heritage and Politics

No future without (remembering) the past. Above all, one must have courage in living up to this principle, and all the more so when one's past is not comfortable or pleasant.

The prosecution and punishment of members of the NSDAP commenced immediately after the war, very much at the insistence of the victorious Allied powers. Some 600,000 Austrians, or about one twelfth of the population, were registered as national socialists in the context of the so-called penance legislation, or *Sühnegesetzgebung.* About 100,000 people were dismissed from their posts in the public service; almost as many were barred from exercising their professions. Forty three death sentences were handed down by the people's courts, of which thirty were carried out. Twenty nine people were sentenced to life sentences, and 269 were sentenced to terms of imprisonment exceeding ten years each.

Former Nazis were disenfranchised, and precluded from taking part in the first free post-war elections held in Austria in 1945; this preclusion did not, however, apply to members of their families. The Austrian People's Party (ÖVP), a right-of-centre Christian democratic party, emerged from the election as the largest party, with almost 50% of all the votes cast. A possible contributory factor to this result was an election poster issued by Erwin Scharf, who was General Secretary of the Austrian Socialist Party (SPÖ) at the time and was later an official of the Austrian Communist Party (KPÖ). The poster read,

> "Tens of thousands of Austrians are currently far from their homeland in prisoner-of-war camps and are badly needed for the reconstruction of Austria. Tens of thousands of Nazis are living in Austria and are sabotaging the reconstruction of Austria. We demand a swap."

Very soon it became clear that the large number of sympathisers of Nazism, the so-called "less incriminated" would have to be reintegrated into society. This was also very much an objective of the Western Allies and a main aim of their 'Re-Education Programme'. A policy of exclusion would not have been sustainable in the long run. It was thus inevitable that all parties, including the Communists, would attempt to woo this segment of the electorate as soon as they were permitted, once more, to take part in the normal political process. This happened in the general election of 1949 and the race for the votes of the national socialists was won, hands down, by the Austrian People's Party (ÖVP).

Although the Communist Party was included in the government of national unity which was formed following the election of 1945, their members quit the government in 1947 over a dispute concerning the currency reform which saw the reintroduction of the schilling for the *Reichsmark*. As the dwindling number of communist members of parliament demonstrated even at the time, this party never succeeded in gaining much popular support among the population. The strike of October 1950, which was a protest action led by shop stewards against sharp price increases following the currency reform, is sometimes represented as an attempted coup by communist sympathisers, and similar to coup attempts in other neighbouring countries. Although the coup hypothesis is treated with scepticism today, the risk was real in the unstable political climate of the times. There were attempts to broaden the strike action by crippling public transport, thus preventing other workers from getting to work, and even embryonic plans existed to storm the chancellor's office and topple the government.

The strike obtained no support from the Soviet zone, and collapsed in the face of resolute opposition from the Building and Woodworkers' Union, led by their chairman, Franz Olah and supported by the CIA. Franz Olah had spent the war years from 1938–45 in Dachau and Buchenwald and was to have a chequered career in the trade union movement, newspapers and the Austrian Socialist Party (SPÖ). In addition to Olah, both the mayor of Vienna, Theodor Körner and the vice-chancellor, Adolf Schärf also played important roles in defeating the strike.

The policy of excluding former registered Nazis from all aspects of political, economic and social life began slowly to be relaxed in the post-war years. This process was accelerated by the commencement of the cold war. The war on communism, which took off as governments in the soviet sphere of influence were toppled one-by-one and replaced by communist regimes, came to a climax with the victory of Mao in China, the Korean War and the mass hysteria of the McCarthy era in the United States itself. The United States quickly came to recognise the Nazis as uncompromising and reliable anti-communists and to view them as the lesser of two evils.

We can take the former SS-espionage chief Wilhelm Höttl as a prominent Austrian example of a former Nazi who was reactivated as an anti-communist weapon by the Americans. He was given a villa in Gmunden, Upper Austria, from where he was charged with resurrecting his former network of SS agents and to deploy them against the East. This change in the international political climate was a major reason why a number of Nazis, several carrying serious burdens of guilt for their wartime activities, successfully managed to slip through the cracks of the people's courts and the denazification process. One such person was Dr. Heinrich Gross, the "euthanasia doctor" stationed at the Viennese children's clinic *am Spiegelgrund* in 1944. Many years later as an old man, his past finally caught up with him when he was charged with the murder of nine handicapped children and suspected of involvement in the murder of many, many more.

At the beginning of 2005, a study appeared which had been commissioned by the Federation of Socialist Academics (BSA), supposedly to analyse and come to terms with the past. This study, which was titled *Der Wille zum aufrechten Gang* (The Will to Stand Upright) can scarcely be said to have lived up to its title; the courageous reappraisal of our history turned out to be exceedingly superficial. This study was highly selective in its coverage and took little or no account of the circumstances or the background which influenced events. Far too much attention was afforded to unsubstantiated presumptions, a methodology which casts serious doubt on the scientific merit of the work. The study took no account of the current political situation nor, indeed, of any possible political fall-out.

It is bordering on the absurd to raise questions and doubts about the personal integrity of such leading personalities as Adolf Schärf, Karl Waldbrunner, the centenary of whose birth we celebrated at the end of 2006, Oskar Helmer, Bruno Kreisky, Christian Broda, or Herta Firnberg. Without exception, these people had shown great courage and provided invaluable public service during the "smutna", i.e.

the time of uncertainty and confusion covering the period of Austro-fascism, the supremacy of the national socialists and the post-war Allied occupation. What can be judged as particularly inappropriate was the dim-witted, brazen malice with which some conservative elements in particular responded to the publication of the BSA study. The claim of some ÖVP-grandees, that their party did not have any "brown stains", is downright absurd. The attitude of the socialist academics, grandchildren of the SPÖ founders, in this affair is nothing short of embarrassing.

The events of the Nazi period in Austria cannot be understood properly without taking careful cognizance of the preceding period of Austro-fascism. And, this concerns the conservative ÖVP very closely. As Hubert Pfoch, a former president of the Vienna provincial parliament, pointedly and succinctly summed up the key issue: In the First Republic, the conservatives first locked up the socialists and the fascists; then, the fascists locked up the conservatives and the socialists. But the socialists were always among the persecuted. The socialists, for their part, never imprisoned their opponents nor incarcerated them in concentration camps.

It took the horror of the Nazi era, the Second World War and the occupation to achieve a reconciliation between the two main opponents of the First Republic, the People's Party and the Socialists. While sharing a common fate in the concentration camps, they managed to climb out of their ideological trenches and forge a common way forward. In the Second Republic, the predominant form of government has been a coalition between these two parties. But the price of this consensus has been a suppression of our history prior to 1938.

At the end of the war, it was not without reason that the Allies set about pursuing not only the Nazis, but also the leaders of Austro-fascism. The "automatic arrest list" which was conducted by the Counter-Intelligence Corp (CIC) included the names of the leaders of the conservative militias (*Heimwehr*), which in their time had been active as defense units of the conservative bourgeoisie, alongside the names of leading Nazis. The leaders of the militias were classified as fascists of the same ilk as the national socialists. It soon transpired that this demand was excessive and could not be carried out, as several members of the government, such as the former concentration-camp inmate, Figl, would also have had to be arrested.

In the interest of safeguarding the new peace agreement between the SPÖ and the ÖVP, it was necessary to suspend the prosecution of a great many leading ÖVP politicians. And, it also meant that any discussion of the Austro-fascist era or its origins was strictly taboo, an implicit arrangement which lasts to this day. The Second Republic has been built upon a cooperative arrangement between the SPÖ and the ÖVP. The foundation of this accommodation has been a democratic consensus, which includes a tacit agreement that the national socialist past will be kept out of all discussion.

As for the ÖVP, a careful examination of the party's history and of the background of its members is very much needed. I would just like to allude to the fact that one of my predecessors as minister for finance in the *Himmelpfortgasse* in Vienna had been an illegal Nazi. Moreover, on 28 May 1949, a meeting of leading ÖVP politicians and former high-ranking members of the NSDAP took place; the meeting was held at Schloss Oberweis in Upper Austria, the castle residence of the ÖVP grandee, Dr. Maletta, and the purpose of the meeting was to discuss the rehabilitation of former members of the nationalist-socialist party. This was also very much a wish and a concern of the one time militia leader and subsequent State-Treaty chancellor, Leopold Figl. The banner headline of the *Kurier* newspaper on 11 June, 1949 proclaimed, "Graf announced: ÖVP insists on the integration of former Nazis in a right wing".

An in-depth coming-to-terms with one's own past is both sensible and necessary. It should not, however, degenerate into an obsessive white-washing exercise or a mania for purity. It is simply not logically possible to control, or change the past; what we must seek to manage is the present, and the future.

It is also necessary for other countries to come to terms with, and analyse, their own behaviour, both before and during the Nazi era. One should not forget that the western powers never paid much attention to, or even really cared about, Austria in the period following the short-sighted, ill-fated and imposed Treaty of Saint-Germain. They failed miserably to react to the unrest and upheaval of the years 1933 and 1934, and failed to respond to the extinction of Austria in March 1938.

Forgiveness Yes – But Never Forget!

Every attempt to analyse or reconcile the past must make allowances for certain individuals and avoid blanket judgements which imply that one measure of guilt fits all. In particular, we must make allowances for those who on grounds of youthful enthusiasm, or innocence, were easily misled. Another group which should not have to bear the full burden of responsibility is the "army" of tacit supporters, those who were mainly concerned with living their lives under whatever circumstances they faced, but who were not an integral part of events. These groups, and others, have very little to feel guilty about. Their change of heart, their conversion and their new sense of direction ought to be respected.

This tolerance was never shown to Friedrich Peter, the leader of the Austrian right-wing Liberal Party who, as a 17 year old in 1938, had joined the NSDAP and had served in the war as an *Obersturmführer* (similar to Lieutenant First Class) in the *Waffen-SS.* The animosity and intolerance towards Peter makes it all the more difficult to comprehend the motivation in awarding Wilhelm Höttl the *Großes Ehrenzeichen des Landes Steiermark*, the highest civic honour the provincial government can award, on 11 July 1995. Höttl had served as the head of espionage in the *Waffen-SS*, and this honour was bestowed largely at the instigation of the ÖVP.

Following the fall of the Franco regime in 1975 in Spain, the young leader of the socialist movement Felipe Gonzales announced that there would be "no crusade of revenge against the Falangists". This was particularly magnanimous when one recalls that the Falange had been the sole authoritarian political force allowed under the rule of Generalissimo Franco and had been especially unsympathetic towards any form of socialism. It was not without reason that the fledgling democrats in the new states of the former Soviet Empire were tolerant towards the old guard of communist functionaries, and offered them an opportunity of rehabilitation.

In this context, I would like to recall the great social-democratic politician, Rosa Jochmann, from whom we inherited the slogan and moral signpost, "Forgiveness yes – but never forget!" And just because circumstances and the ethos of the times have changed and the passage of time may have softened our focus, there is absolutely no reason to treat the history of the corporatist state during the period of Austro-fascism in the same casual manner as one might, say, the lifetime of the Empress Elizabeth, or Sisi as she is popularly known. This would amount to a complete loss of historical perspective, of the relative significance of different historical episodes. It would be unhelpful, to say the least, and would even be provocative in glossing over a violent regime which was morally and politically bankrupt.

It can be highly detrimental to those who are out of favour and seeking rehabilitation, to have self-righteous and self-serving hypocrites sitting in judgement, and handing down verdicts with complete disregard for the personal or political damage they may cause. People do not act in a vacuum, and their actions can only be evaluated and judged in the context of the political and social circumstances of their day. And, for exactly the same reason, we will have to consider all the circumstances when we seek to write the history of the First and Second Republics. In no sense can we ignore, or exclude, the topics of political persecution, victims, resistance and forced emigration which occurred in the years of Austro-fascism. And neither can we ignore the history of those who were "rehabilitated" without any form of public acceptance or public atonement.

One of the many who returned was Otto Binder, a former general manager of the *Wiener Städtische*, the Vienna Insurance Group, a state-owned insurance company. His final publication, which appeared posthumously, described the career of Rudolf Neumayr as head of the *Wiener Städtische* during the time of the Nazis. As Binder described him,

Neumayr was "willing to serve all masters" and a "collaborator". During the Schuschnigg government, which followed the assassination of Dollfuß, Neumayr served as minister for finance. When Hitler invaded Austria in 1938, Neumayr served the Nazis and even received the highest honour the NSDAP could bestow, the *Goldenes Parteiabzeichen*, despite the fact that he had never been a party member.

So far as we can tell, Binder's motive in publishing this account had nothing to do with revenge, or with settling old scores. Instead, his objective was to show future generations what it was like to live, and survive in those turbulent times. Most people were not committed to whichever faction or ideology was in power and simply wanted to get on with their lives. They learned to adapt to changing governments, no matter how radically different they might be. Adaptation was the key to survival. Today, the Nazis have been demonised, and rightly so. But then, and for most people, it was just another political change to which ordinary people had to adapt to survive – like so often before.

Personal Recollections of Historical Events

In reflecting on those dark times of Austro-fascism and the Second World War, many fragments of personal recollection come into mind.

My attitudes to the crutch cross, a variant of the Jerusalem cross and predominant symbol of Dollfuß's Fatherland Front, no less than the Nazi swastika, are well known and need not be elaborated upon here. As a person I am very much guided by intuition and pay careful attention to my feelings on various issues, without ever presuming to set myself up as a judge of others. But, I am deeply convinced that it is possible for individuals who have followed some erroneous path, to change and reform, both morally and politically; how genuine this conversion really is can only be evaluated on an individual basis. On this issue I find myself at odds with a great many people. And Friedrich Peter is a good example of this as I am unshakably convinced of the sincerity of his conversion.

I grew up in a social democratic family which was decidedly anti-fascist, anti-communist and anti-national socialist. Our family also had quite a tradition of political involvement and activity. My great-grandfather took part in the first May parade in 1890 which was organised in the Prater Park in Vienna. Georg Sailer, a great uncle on my mother's side of the family, stood for election to the *Reichsrat*, or Imperial Council of the Austrian Empire until 1918. After the fall of the monarchy, he became a member of the *Bundesrat* (Federal Council), the senate or upper house of parliament, as well as a member of the *Nationalrat* (National Council), the lower house of the national parliament.

My maternal grandfather was imprisoned on 12 February 1934 along with his friend, Hans Hornschall. On that day, the Dollfuß government sought to disarm the *Republikanischer Schutzbund*, the militia of the Socialist Workers Party, and the government's attempt to storm a party building in Linz was the starting shot of a brief, if bloody, civil war. Hans Hornschall was subsequently rehabilitated, and died in 1943 in the Nazi resistance movement. However, in 1934, my parents' council apartment in the *Freytaggasse* on the *Alte Donau* waterfront suffered extensive damage as it was the target of artillery fire from the opposite bank of the Danube. Four years later, they narrowly escaped having their apartment confiscated by the Nazis.

My father also took part in what was one of the final attempts to resist a national socialist takeover. On 7 March 1938, less than one week before the German invasion, he participated in a meeting in Floridsdorf which was organised by the trade union movement. Throughout the war, he secretly tuned in to Radio Beromünster, the independent Swiss radio station, and tracked the progress of the war by marking the shifting front-lines on a map of Europe which he had nailed to the door of our living room. Even as a very young child I had a pretty good idea what to think of the Nazis, judging by how they were spoken of at home. Nevertheless, I can clearly remember how, as a five year old and much to the annoyance of my family, I used to get a kick out of parking myself across from the flak barracks near our home and greeting every uniformed person who passed by with the Hitler salute. This continued until, one day, I was escorted by two members of the Hitler Youth to a nearby field, where one of them forced me at the point of a drawn dagger to eat grass and clay.

As a seven year old in 1945, I experienced the expulsion of my relatives from Priesling in the southern part of Moravia. They were part of the German-speaking population of the "*Sudetenland*" which was accused of collaboration with the Nazi war effort. Without any evidence whatsoever, and without legal process or any form of compensation, some three million people were dispossessed and expelled from what is now the Czech Republic. We had fled from the bombing attacks on Vienna and had gone to live with our relatives in the comparative safety of Moravia. At the time, my mother was heavily pregnant. Still, she brought me to the window to watch the desolate cavalcade pass by, and said; "You must look out at this and never forget it for all of your life".

My mother, my new-born sister, my father and I returned later to Vienna. Because of a serious deformity of the spine, my father had been classified as unfit for active service, and had thus avoided conscription into the army. We now found that the Russians had occupied the neighbouring flak-barracks and that a Russian officer was quartered in my parental home. He was a civil engineer and was working on the rebuilding of the Floridsdorf Bridge across the Danube. The Russians had renamed the bridge after one of their war heroes, Marshall Malinowsky. You could now tell the political attitude of tram drivers when they came to the bridge tram-stop by whether they announced the stop as Floridsdorf bridge or Malinowsky bridge.

A close friend of the family, the medical doctor Dr. Rudolf Steiner, managed to emigrate to England. At first he was interned by the British and during his incarceration in the internment camp he contracted a debilitating lung ailment. His parents, who had been looked after by my grandmother until shortly beforehand, were deported, and died in a concentration camp. Dr. Steiner later summed up his predicament with the observation that, in the eyes of the Italians, he was an Austrian pig, the Nazis regarded him as a Jewish pig, and the British viewed him as a German pig.

My father also brought me along to the homecoming celebration for Karl Seitz when he returned from internment in the *Ravensbrück* concentration camp. Seitz had been an illustrious social democrat for more than half a century. During his tempestuous career, he had served as party leader of the parliamentary socialist party, as deputy speaker of parliament, and, briefly, as head of state during the First Republic. However, it was during his twelve years as provincial governor and mayor of Vienna that he really left his mark; during this time, enlightened policy innovations in the fields of health, finance and education had made Vienna an international model of social democratic governance. Following the civil war of February 1934, he was removed from office and imprisoned by the Dollfuß government.

Although a relatively old man when he returned from wartime incarceration, I still remember clearly his jubilant homecoming, which was held in the building complex in Floridsdorf which still bears his name. This return, along with many others, marked the end of the war and the advent of liberation. From this wanton destruction emerged a new beginning and a new start. It would still take some time until liberation would become freedom, or until shortages would disappear and turn to prosperity and a higher quality of life. Gone were the dark years of war and persecution with their associated threats and the burden of occupation. Few could have imagined that we were at the dawn of more than sixty years of freedom and security.

Individuals who experienced the post-war years of austerity and deprivation will no doubt have their own personal recollections of this time. I would like to recount a colourful and memorable experience of an acquaintance of mine, which I am sure will be of interest even to the youth of today who have never experienced hardship or want. The story dates from the late 1940s and early 1950s, when this friend's parents tended their own garden in a rural part of Carinthia in the south of Austria. Every week, they brought the produce of their own garden to the local market. There they could stare at exotic fruit, such as bananas, which were on sale at an exorbitant price, but which were as far out of reach as the stars in the sky. It was only when single bananas had begun to go off in a couple of places were they offered for sale as appetisers, and it was only in this form that they were available as an affordable delicacy.

It is equally difficult to imagine today the emotional impact with which the Austrian population experienced their first steps to freedom, the first parliamentary elections, and the signing of the State Treaty which signalled an end to Allied occupation. My brother in law, Professor Dr. Schneider remembers clearly how, like many others, he was allowed to accompany his grandfather to the polling booth on election day; it was a festive occasion for which one had to dress in their Sunday best. The 15 May 1955 resonates memorably in my recollections, as I went by tram to St. Stephen's Square to join the multitudes there. The crowds had assembled to witness the ringing of the "*Pummerin*" to proclaim the signing of the State Treaty. (The "*Pummerin*" is the legendary bell on St. Stephen's Cathedral which is only rung on very special occasions).

The Second Republic: The State Everyone Wanted

At the end of the Second World War the country was in ruins and facing ruin. But there was a significant difference between the mood of the country at this time and that prevailing at the end of the First World War. In the final days of April 1945, people faced the future with a measure of hope and a confidence that a new Austria could emerge from the rubble heap that had once been the "Third Reich".

In the early summer of 1943, the future Austrian president Adolf Schärf had asked Wilhelm Leuschner what the future was likely to bring for Austria after the end of Hitler's regime. Leuschner, a stalwart social democrat and trade unionist and inveterate opponent of national socialism, had served as interior minister in the federal state of Hesse prior to Hitler usurping power in Germany in 1933; he was hanged after the failed assassination attempt on Hitler on 20

July 1944 in which he was a likely candidate for the position of vice-chancellor. Prophetically, his reply to Schärf's question was that: "The *Anschluss* is dead. The desire of many Austrians for a German *Reich* has been well and truly exorcised".

The attempt to rebuild Austria out of the rubble and ash commenced with great determination in 1945. There was no doubting the universal will to re-establish freedom and the Austrians' resolution to be master in their own house once more. This struggle for freedom, the exertions in effecting the withdrawal of the forces of occupation and the harnessing of the reconstruction effort, all contributed to a new self-confidence and national self-awareness. After 1945, and by 1955 at the latest, Austria became a nation which its citizens very much longed for.

Austria had once more discovered its sense of identity, its individuality and integrity as a nation, and this was clearly perceptible in the provinces, the political parties and also in the various interest groups which were active at the time. The traumatic experiences of the First Republic, the Third Reich and the Second World War, were pushed into the background as it were, and superseded by the feeling of communal success emanating from the reconstruction and the signing of the State Treaty on 15 May 1955. This treaty, which was the final act in the post-war occupation of the Allied forces, meant that Austria had, finally, gained its full independence.

One has to be realistic and realise that the State Treaty was concluded because it somehow met the interests of the Allied occupying powers; as a pawn on the great chess board of World politics, Austria's interests were of secondary importance. Nevertheless, this coincidence of the interests of all parties involved enabled Austria to exploit this brief window of opportunity to reach out and grasp its freedom.

The neutrality of Austria was an important condition associated with this treaty although not actually incorporated into the treaty document. The primary objective of this requirement was to ensure Austrian neutrality in the Cold War between East and West and, in the context of the times, was a perfectly reasonable precondition. Nevertheless, neutrality has progressed in the minds of many, from a pragmatic instrument of political expediency to an institution which is an integral part of our national identity. But, the conditions which gave rise to our neutrality no longer exist, and such a status is not envisaged, either in the context of the United Nations, or within the European Union. In the future, Austria will have to play its part in the Union, and will not be able to avoid the responsibility which each individual member state carries with respect to common security and foreign policy.

As the Second Republic became increasingly integrated into the western economic system, it gradually changed the focus of its foreign and economic policies. Historically, Austria has always looked towards East and Southeast Europe, a region it has strongly influenced and in return received considerable influence from. Driven by the Soviet dominance in Eastern Europe and even more so by the creation of the "iron curtain", Austria's orientation shifted gradually, if increasingly, towards the West. Membership of the OECD, the Council of Europe, GATT and other international bodies was a logical consequence of this change. However, these were all institutions premised on the principle of international cooperation.

Until the Soviet Empire collapsed in the late 1980s, Austria felt itself contractually and legally restricted by the neutrality clause in the State Treaty from joining international entities with a political dimension. This mood changed in the early 1990s as the changing political landscape in Europe rendered such a restrictive clause outdated and obsolete. In 1994, Austria joined the European Economic Area and on 1 January one year later became a full member of the European Union. Since then it has taken part in many international agreements as part of the EU and has introduced the new European currency, the euro. All of these changes have helped to make Austria an integral part of a greater European clan.

From the Poor House to Prosperity

If Austria was regarded as a poor-house in the period between the wars, this was even more the case at the end of the Second World War. Half a century later, it would be counted amongst the most prosperous countries in the world. The Second Republic has thus very much been an economic success story, and this assertion does not require any doctoring of history to bear it out. In his book, *Wirtschaft und Wirtschaftspolitik nach dem Zweiten Weltkrieg* (The Economy and Economic Policy since the Second World War), which appeared in 2005, Hans Seidl provides the essential empirical details.

This success story might seem all the more remarkable when one considers the unfavourable initial conditions; in particular, the remarkable number of war victims and the extensive destruction. In spite of everything, and notwithstanding the generous financial support provided by the American Marshall Programme, the burden of recovery was enormous. Significant hindrances which should not be underestimated were the restrictions and suffering of ten further years of foreign occupation and, of course, the outbreak of the Cold War, which left the world divided into two inimical camps, with Austria in no-man's-land, perched on the perimeter of the "Iron Curtain".

For all of that, Austria's economic prosperity after the war progressed in rapid steps. The first phase has been called the period of "pragmatic improvisation" by Stephan Koren. It covers the three years from 1945 to 1947 and was characterised by chaos, hunger, pent-up inflation and a veritable struggle for survival. Economic policy was restricted to ensuring provision of the bare essentials – regulating production, distribution through rationing, and the centralised setting of prices. In a real sense, we had a command economy.

In 1946 and 1947, Austria saw an extensive nationalisation of the raw-materials industries, electricity production and the banks. These measures had little to do with ideological conviction and were entirely based on pragmatic considerations. As these industries had officially belonged to Nazi Germany following the invasion of 1938, this "nationalisation" device helped to keep them from falling into the hands of the Allied powers as spoils of war. At the same time, it helped to secure the supply of resources and materials which were central to the reconstruction effort. Some time later, the so-called "German assets" were legally re-patriated, and the Western allies handed this property back to the newly re-established Austrian state.

The second phase of economic reconstruction, covering the period of 1947 to 1952, started with a currency reform. This coincided with the introduction of the Marshall Plan, from which Austria derived enormous benefit. The Plan, which offered financial assistance for reconstruction work to all countries suffering from the aftermath of the war, was not accepted by any of the Eastern European countries falling within the Soviet sphere of influence. Of the countries which did accept assistance, Austria came out top of the beneficiaries' league when measured on a *per capita* basis. Economic recovery continued rapidly, so that by the beginning of 1949, basic staples no longer had to be rationed.

In spite of the currency restrictions of 1947, all efforts at bringing the money supply under control failed, and led to an alarming acceleration in the inflation rate. This continued with worrying implications into the year 1952, the year in which the Korean War ended and in which the four-year US-aid programme in the context of the Marshall Plan also came to an end. An uncontrollable inflation rate carried the risk of destabilising the economy and jeopardising economic recovery. As a result, a programme of extensive financial cutbacks was introduced by the government of the day, under the guidance of the finance minister, Reinhard Kamitz, and in response to enormous pressure exerted by the Americans.

This economic reform programme was highly successful and was subsequently, and cleverly, billed by the ÖVP, the People's Party, as the "Raab-Kamitz Plan" in their election campaign of 1956. However, this attempt to credit the chancellor of the day, Julius Raab, with the success of this policy was more than misleading. In the course of private discussions with the parties involved, I have first-hand confirmation that the true architects of the plan were finance minister Kamitz in close cooperation with Karl Waldbrunner, then minister for transport and the nationalised industries. It would have been more appropriate to present this policy as the "Kamitz-Waldbrunner Plan".

The international debt treaty, concluded in Rome in 1952, also made a significant contribution to the recovery in Austria. Under the terms of this treaty, the crippling burden of Austria's pre-War debts was dramatically reduced. The phase of economic recovery was concluded on 27 July 1953 with the final abolition of food rationing. This was accompanied by a period of liberalisation of internal markets and the fixing of the schilling-dollar exchange rate at 1.26, an unmistakable sign of renewed confidence in the stability of the economy and the financial system.

The appearance that trade between countries was making significant steps towards liberalisation was deceptive. The pegged exchange-rate system, introduced under the auspices of the International Monetary Fund, was only sustainable because it was backed up by stringent exchange controls, which all but precluded significant and "undesirable" capital flows between countries. In Europe, exchange controls were to remain in operation until they were abolished in the early 1990s in preparation for monetary union. Competition in markets for goods and services was severely restricted by high and variable tariff barriers, not to mention a partly-visible plethora of non-tariff barriers. The General Agreement on Tariffs and Trade, known as GATT, was established to address the problem of tariffs, but progress was slow.

Significant progress in the liberalisation of trade and payments, in Europe, was to await the creation of the EEC and EFTA in the late 1950s and early 1960s. What we now describe as European integration can be seen as a phase of economic liberalisation and elimination of restrictions, combined with a layer of supra-national political control. That the reach of the Brussels administration now extends so far into the daily life of the member states, is a reflection of the complexity and difficulty in arranging a "level playing field" in international trade and payments.

Steps Towards European Integration

The essential measures in the creation of a modern industrial state in Austria were in place by 1953 and, from then on, the Austrian economy blossomed into a well-functioning market economy. Of course, as was universal in the aftermath of the war, this "free" market was supplemented by a large measure of state intervention, epitomised by the nationalised industries. Following the phase of post-war reconstruction in the late 1940s and early 1950s, the Second Republic embarked on a period of sustained economic growth, which commenced in 1955 and which continued almost without interruption for two decades until 1974/75.

During this period, European economic integration was progressing with astonishing rapidity. The foundation was laid in 1952 with the establishment of the European Coal and Steel Community (the ECSC), which was legally created under the Treaty of Paris. Under the terms of this treaty, the six member-countries, comprised of France, Italy and West Germany, along with the three smaller Benelux countries, agreed to establish a supra-national framework, or Community, to manage their combined coal and steel industries. Management and operational decisions were taken out of the hands of the member-country governments and placed under the control of an elaborate array of supra-national institutions, which were termed "the Community". This extraordinary structure, which contained *inter alia* a parliament and a supra-national court, was considered necessary to facilitate the re-establishment and development of these most strategically vital national industries. Probably in no other way could the understandable mistrust and mutual suspicion have been overcome between countries which, a few years earlier, had waged the most murderous war in history on each other.

The success of the ECSC led to the suggestion that this arrangement could beneficially be extended into other spheres of economic co-operation. Some six years after the Treaty of Paris, this process came to fruition with the signing of the Treaty of Rome, of which there were, in reality, two. What we know today as *the* Treaty of Rome led to the establishment of the European Economic Community (or, EEC) in 1958. It envisaged the coordination of economic policy in a wide range of economic sectors, across the member countries, with particular importance attached to transport and agriculture. The second, and less well known, Treaty of Rome, led to the creation of a Nuclear Energy Community (or, EURATOM), which was dedicated to the peaceful exploitation of nuclear energy. Legally, we then had three separate Communities, the ECSC, the EEC, and EURATOM. This situation was partly rationalised in 1967 when the EEC and EURATOM were fused into a single community, the European Community (or, EC); in 1992, the EC was transformed into the European Union (or, EU). The ECSC came to an end in 2002 – the treaty had been entered into for a fifty-year period – and the decision not to extend it beyond 2002 meant that coal and steel reverted to the status of economic sectors within the EU.

Austria could not take part in this historic process. Austrian neutrality, as enshrined in the *Neutralitätsgesetz 1955* (Neutrality Act) following the State Treaty of 1955, precluded the country's participation in any form of supra-national political integration, which the EEC clearly was. The Cold War made the situation even more intractable. The Allied powers, which were signatories to the State Treaty, and the Soviet Union in particular, would never have accepted Austrian membership of the EEC. Ironically, the political dimension was also Britain's fundamental problem with the EEC and the main cause of Britain's reluctance to join the new organisation at inception. Later, the closeness of Britain's relations with the United States was a factor in France's reluctance to have Britain as a member. Following de Gaulle's infamous veto in 1960, which closed the door to British membership of the EEC (and later EC) for the next thirteen years, the British Government set up a trade block which was devoid of a political dimension. This was called the European Free Trade Association, or EFTA, and Austria became one of its founding members along with Norway, Sweden, Denmark and Portugal. They were later joined by Switzerland, Finland, Liechtenstein and Iceland.

This arrangement by no means solved Austria's economic problems. Top of the list was the fact that Austria's largest neighbours and trading partners, West Germany and Italy, were members of the EC. The barrier between Austrian and West German markets was particularly disadvantageous, as trading links with Germany had traditionally been very close. This threatened to become even more disadvantageous in the early 1970s when Great Britain, Denmark, Ireland and Norway applied for EC membership, with the first three mentioned attaining membership status in 1973. The special needs of Austria were recognised, and partly resolved, in 1972, with the signing of a bilateral trade agreement between Austria and the EC, which effectively led to free trade in industrial goods.

The picture changed dramatically and rapidly when Mikhail Gorbachev became general secretary of the Communist Party of the Soviet Union in 1985. His policies of reform (*perestroika)*, openness (*glasnost*) and acceleration of economic development (*uskoreniye*) led to a gradual reappraisal of the hindrances to Austrian membership of the EC. On 19 June 1989, the Austrian parliament authorised the government to initiate negotiations with the EC with a view to attaining full membership of that organisation. It was felt that the end of the Cold War and the collapse of the Soviet Union created a changed situation, which rendered the old restrictions redundant and now made membership conceivable. Following conclusion of the Treaty of Accession with the EU, the Austrian people emphatically endorsed membership in a public referendum, with a vote of 66.4%. Austria finally became a member country of the EU on 1 January 1995.

Social Change and Ideological Conflict

Advances in technology and the emergence of a new system of cultural values were not the only innovative features to characterise the 1960s and 70s. The introduction of microprocessors and computers were in the forefront of the transition from an industrial age to a new age of information and a knowledge-based society. Advances in the sphere of diagnostic technology, in addition to transplantation- and micro-surgery, set new and hitherto undreamt-of standards in medical treatment.

The traditional social order, and in particular the role of women in this order, experienced a dramatic upheaval through the impact of the feminist movement and the widespread use of the birth-control pill. Society was also transformed by a sequence of other developments which were to exert a lasting effect on commercial and social life; foremost amongst them, one could list the shortening of the standard working week, the emergence of a leisure industry, global tourism, greater access to health and education services, greater life expectancy and the dramatic decline in the birth rate, with the consequential modification of the population pyramid. The emergence of this new age was characterised by a decoupling of the working hours of men from that of machines. Knowledge became increasingly important as a factor of production. Intellectual power took precedence over muscle power; brain became more important than brawn.

The economic development of the immediate post-war period can be regarded as a euphoric stage of national reconstruction and rediscovery. But very soon a sentiment of soul-searching and self-questioning emerged, which posed the questions where this emphasis on economic growth was leading to, and what societal priorities it represented?

This emerging protest movement questioned the appropriateness of setting materialistic objectives, combined with authoritarian structures, as the primary goals in life. The movement also rejected the meaningfulness of technical progress, given that not every technical advance can be counted as progress. This was, in effect, a challenge to the well-known Schumpeterian aphorism whereby technical progress is viewed as "creative destruction". Joseph A. Schumpeter, one of the most celebrated of all Austrian economists, was inclined to emphasise the "creative" nature of technical progress, as were his capitalistic followers, whereas the protest movement tended to highlight its "destructive" character.

This protest movement culminated in the student revolts of 1968, which originated in Paris but spread rapidly to affect student movements everywhere. But it was more than a protest against the culture and values of the old generation with their emphasis on accepting uncritically the greater wisdom of elected rulers, or elders, and viewing self-sacrifice in the common interest as a noble destiny. It questioned fundamentally and critically the wisdom of elected leaders and the decisions they made, the democratic system which produced them, the values they represented, and even the social order they sought to perpetuate. In a patriarchal political environment there is little to be gained from merely changing the government, or even the generation of rulers. One has to reform the political institution itself to make it more responsive to the wishes and needs of individuals, and one has also to change the minds of the electorate.

At the beginning of the 1970s, the Club of Rome published a landmark report titled *The Limits to Growth*, which identified the limited reserves of exhaustible natural resources as the central problem facing mankind. At contemporaneous rates of utilisation, these would soon be depleted with inevitably disastrous consequences. Those projections have proven, in time, to have been far too pessimistic; still, they provided the intellectual basis for a whole new ecological movement, which in turn provided a stimulus to innumerable grass-roots protests and initiatives concerning the environment.

The anti-war protest movement was a manifestation of a new youthful generation rejecting establishment values and perceptions. The cold war, the escalation of the Vietnam war, the succession of wars in the Middle East and, last but not least, the crushing of the "Prague Spring" through "panzer communism" (Ernst Fischer), all contributed to a vehement rejection of what was viewed as a corrupt political hegemony in the vice-like grip of the armaments industry and a self-serving military establishment. This youthful movement proposed love and brotherhood (or sisterhood) instead of war and aggression, an orientation which was encapsulated in the expression "flower power". Their epoch-defining slogan, "make love not war" was an effective and powerful polemical counterweight to ideological or political arguments in favour of war.

By the late 1980s, the protest movement had lost much of its idealistic fervour. Disaffected youth, many beginning life with insurmountable educational and social disadvantages, now tended to drop out of the "rat race" and reject what they viewed as a "yuppie culture" of striving for a lucrative career and social status. On the other hand, a materialistic society regarded them as "social scroungers", living off welfare benefits they did not deserve and, in a sense, "biting the hand that fed them". The romanticism of the protest movement was over.

The dramatic social changes which occurred between the late 1960s and the late 1980s had other negative consequences. The drugs culture spread like wildfire, and with it the new phenomenon of drugs-related crime. Violent terrorist groups emerged in different countries, with the avowed objective of destroying the capitalist system. The best known were the RAF in Germany and the Red Brigades in Italy, but there were others. These events did not pass Austria by without a trace, but Austria was fortunate indeed to experience them in muted form. It was very much in this context that Pope Paul VI described Austria as the "island of the blessed" in a private audience he held with the Austrian Federal president, Franz Jonas, on 18 November 1971. This description of Austria has now become a dictum.

Hard Currency Policy as a Precursor of the Euro

On 15 August 1971, US president Nixon declared the suspension of the convertibility of the dollar. This was the end of the system of fixed exchange rates, laid down in 1944 in the Bretton Woods Agreement, whereby the dollar had exchanged for gold at $35 per oz, and all other currencies were linked indirectly to gold via the dollar. The convertibility of the US dollar into gold could no longer be sustained as the total stock of dollars outside the US exceeded the capacity of the US to redeem it at the official price. Turbulence on world markets inevitably followed, and Austria coped with this turbulence very successfully by means of its "hard schilling" policy, i.e. by pegging the schilling to the Deutschmark to a large extent. What is still often overlooked, however, is that the schilling had been significantly devalued beforehand against the Deutschmark and the Swiss frank.

The "DMarkisation" of the Austrian currency was based on the theoretical concept by Robert A. Mundell, who taught at Columbia University and was awarded the Nobel Prize in 1999 for his scientific work on the introduction of optimal currency areas.

This currency policy, which effectively anticipated the euro, was initially rejected by industry, above all by the Federation of Austrian Industry and the Federal Economic Chamber; it was opposed politically by the Freedom Party (FPÖ) and the People's Party (ÖVP). Eventually, the finance minister succeeded in implementing this policy, even in the face of opposition from Bruno Kreisky, the finance minister's own head of government. However, it was supported by the Austrian Trade Union Federation (ÖGB) and its president Anton Benya. Karl Waldbrunner, Heinz Kienzl and Georg Albrecht, then senior officials of the Austrian National Bank, were also very supportive.

The conflict described here destroyed the mutual trust between the chancellor and his finance minister; however, their relationship had already been under a cloud for some time due to their strongly diverging views in other areas, such as how to deal with the crisis in the public-sector industries, or how to finance the welfare state.

In October 1973, the first oil price shock rocked the global economy. The economic crisis that followed put an end to the period of extraordinary prosperity after the Second World War, which later became known as the "Golden Age" in the Anglo-American world, or as the "glorious thirty" (*les trentes glorieuses*) in France.

Many regarded the oil crisis as a mere supply issue. At that time, few people realised that it heralded a long-term deterioration of the economic climate. The enterprises of the public industries were particularly affected by this decline: The government opted for a strategy of preserving existing structures rather than carrying out structural adaptations – contrary to the position of the finance minister, whose ministry was not responsible for the state industries. Disaster ensued inevitably. The public enterprises had to be restructured at the expense of 10.9 billion euro, and a loss of 40,000 jobs. However, the reduced influence of the public authorities, as proprietor, did have a positive result in that entrepreneurial responsibility was transferred to the management, thus leading to their subsequent recovery and success.

Later, and not only in Austria, were liberal and neoliberal attitudes to prevail, claiming that the state as an entrepreneur had had its day. A wave of privatisations followed, leading up to the current situation where governments believe that they are forced to privatise state-owned enterprises in order to cap their budget deficits. Austria did not stop short of pointlessly selling off its state-owned property either, as one can see from the fate of the *Tabakwerke* (the formerly state-owned tobacco industries) or *Bank Austria* (the largest Austrian bank).

In its report called "The Limits to Privatisation", Club of Rome member Ernst Ulrich von Weizsäcker provided evidence of the risks we run if essential tasks of the state, especially in the fields of infrastructure and facilities, are transferred to private hands. To give an example, the privatisation of the water supply, a natural monopoly, has failed spectacularly nearly everywhere. Weizsäcker points out that the countries with the fastest economic growth, such as China, India and Japan, are largely state-centred, thus putting the widely prevailing view that growth can only follow on liberalisation, into perspective. In principle, the question "*privat oder Staat*" (private versus public ownership) can only be decided on grounds of efficiency, not according to economic ideologies.

Pragmatic Economic and Fiscal Policy as a Recipe for Success

By means of a series of fiscal and economic policy measures, Austria successfully counteracted the economic slump of 1974/1975, as well as the second oil price shock in 1979. This policy mix, which was not based on any patent remedy, was soon given labels. Depending on one's point of view and focus, this economic policy mix of hard currency policy, budgetary policy and incomes policy, supplemented by stabilisation agreements between the ministry of finance, the National Bank and the credit institutions, was either – somewhat exaggeratedly – labelled "Austro-Keynesianism" (Hans Seidel) or "Austro-Monetarism" (Gottfried Haberler).

In order to support economic activity, a comprehensive public investment programme was implemented, which had a pronounced effect on employment. Expenditure under this programme increased the net budgetary deficit of the Federal state, despite being in balance over the period 1967 to 1972, up to 4.5% of GDP (in 1975 and 1976). This expansionary budgetary policy was followed by a consolidation course, decreasing the net deficit of the Federal state to 2.5% of GDP in 1981. This deficit would have more than met the Maastricht criteria of 1993.

In the 1970s, Austrian growth rates were higher than the European average. At the beginning of this decade, Austria nearly achieved zero-deficits as well as surpluses in the central government balance. The annual average unemployment rate was 2%, the highest number of unemployed was registered in May 1978, amounting to 58,600. Despite the increase in oil prices, the inflation rate remained a single-digit figure. Thanks to the "hard schilling", Austria, along with Germany and Switzerland, was the country with the most stable prices. During this period, Austria pulled itself into the economic fast lane and became "fit for Europe".

A survey (by IMAS in 1998) showed that Austrians were convinced that their country had never been as prosperous as during the last three decades of the 20th century. In the opinion of the adult respondents, the best period was, however, the "golden age" of the 1970s. Many people still remember the dynamic economic development with low unemployment, and the noticeable increase in wealth which they clearly felt at that time.

The Foundations of Social Solidarity

The economic integration of Europe laid the foundations for a peaceful development in Western Europe after the War. European integration and increasing globalisation, as well as worldwide liberalisation and deregulation, mean that it is no longer possible for a country to have its own national economic policy to the same extent as in the past. However, a country like Austria still has considerable scope in shaping its national economy.

The objective of national policy in global competition is to make the national state as attractive an economic location as possible. Some essential factors for achieving that are an outstanding infrastructure, a future-oriented education system, excellent conditions for science and research, an efficient administration, internal and external security, an intact environment, as well as a welfare system assured of a good future.

However, policy also has the task of implementing social solidarity in practice, by means of a democratic social policy based on the four freedoms which Roosevelt referred to in his famous speech – freedom of opinion, freedom of religion, freedom from need, and freedom from fear – and protecting people from what the liberal English social politician Lord Beveridge called the "five evil giants": need, illness, poverty, unemployment, and ignorance.

Today, the demands originally made of the welfare state, a minimum level of social security in the event of illness, invalidity or unemployment, as well as an adequate old age pension, are surpassed by far. In Western Europe in particular, following the reconstruction after the Second World War, prosperity has evolved beyond comparison in history. Eric Hobsbawm rightfully stated that an average citizen in the developed industrialised countries today has better living conditions than a monarch had 200 years ago.

The objective is to create an affluent society as described by John Kenneth Galbraith, offering people a high quality of life as well as financial security. The outdated ideal of the state as a universal provider is redundant because it has reached a point where it can no longer be financed. In addition, it is no longer compatible with individuality, mobility and constant change, all of which characterise today's knowledge society. The basic ideological paradigm of a social and ecological market economy has to aim at as much provision, responsibility and initiative of the individual as possible, and as much intervention by the state as necessary. Providing obligatory and comprehensive benefits "from the cradle to the grave" is neither possible nor desirable, as was once pointed out by Helmut Schmidt and Willy Brandt in their book "*Deutschland 1976: Zwei Sozialdemokraten im Gespräch*" (Germany 1976: Discussions with Two Social Democrats).

An indispensable element of social solidarity in a democracy is the manner in which political parties treat the exercise of power and its transition from one government to another. In view of the troubled relations between the major parties and the social segments they represented between the wars, there was inevitably some residual tension governing their relations, as the controlling influence of the Allied powers was relaxed.

In the immediate post-war period, Austria had a government of national unity in which all factions were represented. Following the State Treaty, Austria was ruled by a "grand coalition" of the People's Party (ÖVP) and the Socialist Party (SPÖ). With the passage of time, the cohesion linking the two largest parties faded and their political viewpoints drifted further apart. From the mid-1960s, the ÖVP ruled alone, and following the election victory of 1970, the Socialists ruled alone for a period of thirteen years.

In their heyday, the two major parties combined shared about 90% of the popular vote. In the 1970s, but especially towards the end of the 1980s, the Freedom Party (FPÖ) emerged as a major force in Austrian politics. This third force has proven to be the "*enfant terrible*" of Austrian politics, with its ultra-nationalist, anti-immigrant pronouncements. On the other hand, the support for the party in the populace at large was such that it could not be ignored.

This realignment in Austrian politics was mirrored at the provincial level. For several decades, the ÖVP held 7 of the 9 provincial governorships or "*Landeshauptleute*", with the SPÖ holding the remaining two. Today the major parties hold four positions each, with the remaining position held by Jörg Haider in Carinthia.

Golden Rules for Stability and Growth

Today, Europe is increasingly losing momentum compared to the US and the growing economic powers in the Far East. The stability criteria laid down in the Maastricht Treaty bind the individual EU member states to a strict budgetary discipline and have turned out to be an obstacle in overcoming this growth crisis. Without any doubt these stability criteria were a necessary reaction to unsound public finances, when from the mid-1980s high debts were incurred all over Europe in order to finance the welfare state, so that the interest charges devoured ever higher tax receipts. This undesirable development had to be corrected, in particular since Keynes' doctrine does not justify this type of "deficit spending".

The current revenue and expenditure of a state should be balanced over a trade cycle, while future-oriented investments could be financed by way of credit, as is also laid down in Article 115 of the Constitution of the Federal Republic of Germany. This "Golden Rule of Public Finances" is also observed by British Treasurer Gordon Brown.

As early as 1878, Lorenz von Stein in his "*Lehrbuch der Finanzwirtschaft*" (Public Finances Textbook), states that, "A state without a state deficit either does too little for its future, or asks too much from its present". Or in other words: A community that incurs too much debt, lives at the expense of its descendants; a community that incurs too little debt, does too little for its descendants.

Preparing a unified single currency area, the EU committed itself to a stability pact in the Maastricht Treaty of 1 November 1993. In the 1997 Treaty of Amsterdam, the Maastricht criteria were supplemented by the obligation to have an active employment policy within the framework of the "Pact for Stability and Growth"; however, the tasks connected with this obligation were neglected, as could soon be seen from the example of trans-European networks. These networks need to be expanded as urgently as Europe needs further future-oriented investments in education and research.

This statement also applies to Austria, where, starting in 1983, but especially since 1986, a huge amount of debt was accumulated, while investments showed a downward trend at the same time; this debt was used above all for financing the increasing expenditure on the welfare state (early retirement pensions, maternity benefit increases, introduction of nursing care insurance) and on the public services. Between 1986 and 1999, the debt of the Federal state increased from 44.8 billion euro to almost 118 billion euro, i.e. by about 73.2 billion euro, or 163%. The political responsibility for this disastrous development lies not only with the Social Democratic Party (SPÖ), which filled the office of the federal chancellor between 1986 and 1999, but also with its coalition partner, the People's Party (ÖVP), which later on claimed credit for the – undoubtedly necessary – correction of this undesirable development.

From 2000, two coalition governments were headed by Wolfgang Schüssel and his People's Party (ÖVP), first with the Freedom Party (FPÖ) and finally with a breakaway faction of the FPÖ, the Alliance for the Future of Austria (BZÖ). The economic policy measures taken by these two coalition governments engaged mainly in "window dressing" and sought only to "embellish" the budget, but did little to reconstruct budgetary policy on a sustained basis. On the contrary: In the year 2001, Austria reached the highest tax rate in its history with 44.8%, and the highest number of registered unemployed people in the Second Republic which averaged 243,880 in 2004. In the same year, Austria also reached a new all-time high of public debt of 150.9 billion euro. These years were also marked by the lowest growth rates of real GDP experienced during the entire period of the Second Republic.

The myth of the "zero deficit" has turned out to be an iridescent soap bubble. The economy is far too complex to enable the use of a single miracle indicator for solving all economic problems. In fact, a pragmatic policy mix is required, targeted at the specific given facts.

If Austria is interested in continuing its success story which began with the Second Republic, and if it wants to pull into the economic fast lane again, then a concerted reform and modernisation initiative is essential, integrating all relevant economic and social-policy players.

In particular, a reform programme will also have to include the federal provinces with their powerful governors, and they will have to make their contribution by slimming-down their administrations, and by adjustments to revenue transfers between the federal state and the provinces. The issue of the *Bundesstaatsreform* (Federal State Reform) is also a typically Austrian curiosity: Under its provisions, the Federal Council, established by the Austrian constitution as the second chamber of Parliament, is of virtually no importance, the informal Conference of the Heads of Provinces (*Landeshauptleutekonferenz*), however, is highly influential. On the other hand, under federal chancellor Schüssel, the institution of the social and economic partnership, which has no legal basis, has lost some of its importance. In the past, it proved to be a tried and tested model for settling conflicts between the employers' and the employees' interests, reflecting the Austrian proclivity for compromise.

Per aspera ad astra: The 20th Century in Europe

It is an extraordinary fact that, in Western Europe today, we can look back on nearly 60 years – that is more than two generations – of peace and increasing prosperity. Europe has always been martial and bloodthirsty and has hardly ever before seen such a long period of time without war in modern history.

The second half of the 20th century differs significantly from the first. For Europe, as for the world, the first half of the century was a cruel and gory period. It was a time of confusion following the carelessly precipitated outbreak of the First World War; the outbreak of the First World War has entered the history books as an example of the "folly of the rulers" (Barbara Tuchman). With Bolshevism and Fascism, further trials and tribulations followed, culminating in the horrors of the Nazi regime, Stalinism, and the Second World War. During this period, Europe's darkest hours were matched by their pendant in the Far East, in the military expansion of Japan.

After the First World War, the gigantic empires of tsarist Russia, the Ottoman Empire and the Empire of the Hohenzollern as well as the Danube Monarchy collapsed. Likewise, the great colonial empires disappeared at the end of the Second World War, pride of place going to the powerful British Empire. Hong Kong, the Empire's last bastion, reverted to China in 1997. As a consequence, Europe lost in importance. For nearly half a century, in the era of the Cold War, Europe was important as a location of strategic interest, until this, too, came to an end with the implosion of the Soviet empire.

Revolutions, Change and Progress

The world has also seen some very profound peaceful changes during the past 60 years. Hardly any sphere of life has been spared these radical changes and globally determined revolutions, most of which have been regarded as progress: Technological developments are allowing science to penetrate the macrocosm and microcosm; medical findings and the latest medical technology are increasing our life expectancy further and further; motorisation is spreading dramatically; telecommunications and mobile communication are shrinking distances; electrification and oil have been supplemented by nuclear energy. Entry into the nuclear age, however, came with a cruel shock: The apocalypse of the atomic bombs dropped on Hiroshima and Nagasaki demonstrated the destructive potential of nuclear weapons. Since then, such weapons have spread further and further. The proliferation of "nukes", and biological and chemical weapons, by no means less dangerous, constitute an enormous world-wide potential threat.

Aviation and space flight have boomed, and new materials have yielded new production processes and skyrocketing output figures; mechanisation and technological progress have affected both agriculture and private households. Industrialisation has reached undreamt-of dimensions, but is nonetheless losing importance in the knowledge age, since knowledge – and thus also education – is becoming an ever more important raw material. The work motto of the future is "inspiration instead of transpiration" (Paul Krugman). Manpower and horsepower are being replaced by brainpower.

In much the same way that people in the 20th century saw entry into a knowledge and information society, the people of the 19th century experienced the change from agricultural society to industrial society. In some countries of the Middle East and Far East, these revolutions are now concentrated within just a few decades. Despite the fact that the number of people employed in agricultural enterprises worldwide keeps decreasing further, agricultural productivity has multiplied, and the agricultural resources we have today would, for all intents and purposes, have the potential to feed the whole of the world's population, i.e. 6.4 billion people. How incredible this development still would have seemed even to progressive America at the beginning of the 20th century, can be illustrated by the following example: When increasing migration into cities and urbanisation caused social problems in the US, a reform movement for modernisation and social justice was formed. It was called the "progressive movement". Theodore Roosevelt was one of its members. The movement's representatives at the time still promised, and prophesied, that in the US there would never be less than 60% of the population employed in agriculture. Today, only 1.8% of US employees work in agriculture; in Europe, the percentage is still 3.7%.

Radio and television introduced the information revolution, now carried on by the widespread application of computers and PCs as well as the Internet. With disappearing geographical barriers and accelerated means of transport and communication, economic activity is extending its scope, mutual relations are becoming closer, and the manifold connections more complex. Borders are becoming more and more penetrable for all sorts of things. These growing global networks and worldwide interdependencies are known to us as "globalisation".

Globalisation and Global Power

In the decade of the 1980s, a new term entered common usage, that of 'globalisation'. At first this expression was associated with economic concerns and problems and, as a result, has been most actively and publicly used as a derogatory slogan by opponents of 'globalisation' ever since. What seems to escape almost everyone's notice, and especially that of the protesters themselves, is that they are coming to an awareness of the phenomenon rather late in the day. Globalisation has been around for rather a long time, as even a most cursory acquaintance with history will quickly reveal. The designation or the expression may be new; not so the phenomenon. In a series of surges over a time period of several centuries, an ever-intensifying and circumfluent network of international contacts has enveloped the globe.

It all began with the overland trade routes, such as the legendary "silk route". But one could not really talk of any serious expansion of intercontinental trade before the late 15th century, after Bartholomew Diaz had succeeded in circumnavigating the southern tip of Africa and his successor, Vasco da Gama, established a sea-route to India in 1498 A.D. In the same year, the Italian-born Spanish explorer, Christopher Columbus, discovered the South American mainland, having discovered the New World six years earlier.

Thereafter, overland routes declined in importance, at least insofar as long distance trade was concerned. The most important commercial routes criss-crossed the oceans, and the world came to be dominated by maritime powers at the expense of nations which were land-based. Political and economic influence depended on an ability to command the high seas and maritime trade routes.

Ironically, China was a great seafaring nation at a much earlier date, but failed to exploit its advantage due to isolationist attitudes. About the year 1440 A.D., during the Ming dynasty, the Chinese even destroyed their astonishing fleet and burned the ships in which Admiral Zheng He had sailed repeatedly to Africa some thirty years before. On board his armada were 30,000 men. In order to get some idea of the extraordinary dimensions of the Chinese ships, any one of them could easily have parked on its deck the three caravels which Columbus sailed in his discovery of the New World.

After the year 1500 A.D., the dominant powers were those which ruled the oceans and progressed to become colonial powers. The first of the great seafaring superpowers were Portugal and Spain; later came Holland and France, and above all, England. It was only when the colonial powers disintegrated in the 20th century that the British Empire was obliged to relinquish its primacy as the global superpower to the United States.

The World We Live in Is Becoming a Global Village

Worldwide networks and international integration have, however, not only developed under the aspect of their economic utilisation. A large number of problems we have today, such as climate change, environmental protection, biodiversity and survival of the species, require a global approach, and thus international cooperation. New global threats require global cooperation; the fight against new diseases such as AIDS or SARS, avian flu or any other risks of pandemics, the fight against international terrorism and international organised crime, or globally dealing with poverty, hunger and social injustice.

Social problems have long been considered and discussed transnationally. Equality of women, for instance, has almost become a global objective, even though it is already comparatively far advanced in the industrialised states. In other parts of the world there is still a lack of awareness of this issue. Problems that require ethical legal solutions also currently concern the developed states of the Free World, and only with a time lag affect global society: stem cell research, euthanasia, the legal equality of same-sex partnerships, as well as contraception or cost allocation for abortions.

Finally, non-governmental organisations, which are increasingly gaining political importance in environmental protection and human rights issues, are also among the positive transnational phenomena.

If we sum up the last decades as periods of change in geopolitical, geo-strategic and geo-economic areas, it is striking above all to see the acceleration with which revolutions, upheavals and structural interruptions occur and tectonic displacements in the geopolitical landscape happen. Two prominent events were already mentioned earlier in this context, the Fall of the Berlin Wall, and the terrorist attack on the Twin Towers in New York. As we know, both events changed the world. A date added to the oft-quoted "nine eleven" memorial day is 11 March, the anniversary of the terrorist attacks on Madrid, which marked the encroachment of global terror into Europe.

September 11 required a new definition of the world order: Until then, sovereignty within national borders – which were also the lines of demarcation of political influence – had applied, at least in principle. But this internationally accepted maxim, as laid down in the Peace of Westphalia of 1648, has become obsolete since September 11 (Henry A. Kissinger). Today we are watching the fields of political action multiply, if not exponentiate. Thus the political subject acting in isolation is becoming much less distinct; in addition to the well-known unit of the nation state, the political players today are also individual regions or peoples, newly formed unions such as for instance the EU, but increasingly also international organisations, enterprises and institutional arrangements.

We will discuss the phenomena of the knowledge revolution and globalisation, but above all the way we deal with them, later. They are an obvious contradiction to the fact that we are currently witnessing the two continents America and Europe drifting apart ideologically.

America and Europe: Incompatible Power Ideologies?

In order to describe the gap between the Old World and the New, the neo-conservative American political scientist, Robert Kagan claimed in his essay on "Power and Weakness" that Americans were from Mars and Europeans were from Venus. This has now become a much cited metaphor. Alluding to the counsellor of couples, John Gray, who used Mars and Venus as an image of the battle between the sexes, Kagan illustrates the different attitude towards power separating the US and Europe ideologically, despite all their conspicuous similarities.

Americans and Europeans live in two different worlds. The Americans currently live in a world in which they rely less and less on international regulations and in which they increasingly base their security and freedom on military power. This world roughly corresponds to the "anarchic natural state" described by the English state philosopher, Thomas Hobbes in the 17th century. The Europeans, on the other hand, have renounced violence and live in a post-historic paradise where conflicts are sorted out peacefully by means of transnational agreements. In Europe's world, Immanuel Kant's ideal of eternal peace seems to have been put into practice. Having said that, we can see how little this image corresponds to European reality, when looking at the real and potential catastrophes on the periphery of Europe, for instance political unrest in the Balkans, that have hardly been resolved to date, in particular in Kosovo, where violence is still lurking and ready to pounce.

However exaggerated this contrasting image of a weapon-dependent cowboy mentality versus a peaceable culture of the meek may be in detail, it still illustrates the current status of an enormous power divide. Actually, the Mars-and-Venus metaphor tells us little about the history of relations between America and Europe. This extended metaphor might be even less appropriate if we examine it in its original context of Greek mythology, where it signifies striving towards reconciliation in harmony. Mars was looking for happiness and contentment in the arms of Venus, with whom he begot Harmonia, mother of the muses and personification of unity and order.

America Puts the World in Order and Rules the Century

As early as February 1941, American media mogul Henry Luce in a leading article in Time Magazine, declared the 20th century to be the "American century" – that was even before Roosevelt agreed with Churchill on founding the United Nations after the Second World War, and above all before the USA had entered the war, following the attack on Pearl Harbour (7 December 1941).

By the beginning of the 20th century, the US was already an important economic power. Its military intervention in the two World Wars determined the outcome of both wars, and the US emerged as a global power from the First World War, and as a superpower from the Second, its only remaining opponent being the Soviet empire. After the Soviet power imploded and collapsed in 1989, the US became the only hyper-power. However, the US is not omnipotent either, and its power can easily turn into ineffectiveness, as was shown by the Vietnam War.

From the perspective of Western Europe, the growing power of the US correlated above all with Europe's dwindling importance. This reality was not altered by the fact that Europe was strategically important during the Cold War, and this geopolitical importance ceased to exist after 1989. During the Cold War, Europe was no longer the subject, but rather an object of world politics. This long period of time has undoubtedly had a soporific effect on the European power instinct, a circumstance which may at least partly explain the lack of European awareness of power which is so often criticised today.

What remains is that we realise that it has only been possible to implement (Western) European peace under the protection of the US. Conflicts smouldered on the other side of the Iron Curtain, breaking out for instance in 1953 in Eastern Germany, in 1956 in Hungary and Poland, in 1968 in Czechoslovakia, and in 1980 again in Poland. Where strong-armed Hobbesian power prevails, it is easy to be a Kantian. The US had to interfere on several occasions in order to protect Europe from itself. Let us remember the Balkans, after the two World Wars, as the most recent example.

Is Transatlantic Unity Breaking Apart?

For a long period of time, economic support in the shape of the Marshall Plan strengthened transatlantic relations, at least in Central European awareness. With the enlargement of NATO, these relations reached a new dimension. On the part of the US, these activities were not motivated solely by altruistic considerations, but were also driven by the US' massive self-interest, not least because this was a strategic interest. Thus, despite progress towards European integration, Europe became a US protectorate. As Egon Bahr said, it became an "unsinkable aircraft carrier".

For the next 50 years, following the attack on Pearl Harbour, Western Europe and the US were allies in the fight against fascism and Nazism, and then again against Bolshevism. This reliable geopolitical axis of the "Free West" perished after their joint enemy had disappeared; the spotlight of the world stage today is not so much on Europe any more, but is focussing on other parts of the world. Europe was one of the main sites of the Second World War, and the central location of the Cold War. As a US protectorate, Europe today is just an "extra" on the international stage in the fight against terrorism. Henry Kissinger sees one reason for the erosion of transatlantic relations in the fact that the generation of political personalities who formed this political axis has now retired. This observation applies to politicians on both sides of the Atlantic. In addition, Kissinger also criticises European statesmen, and justifiably so, for their unhealthy degree of self-centredness: Those in power have somewhat lost their global-policy vision beyond the objective of European integration and the problems connected with it.

Europe is facing the historical decision of whether to become a global player in this power game, or whether to be just the pawn of the global players.

America Rules – Always and Everywhere

At 500 billion US dollars, the US currently accounts for half the world's military expenditure. In 2007, US military expenditure will already amount to more than half, or at least more than the sum total of the military budgets of the 14 next-ranked countries. Not least because it owns 13 aircraft carriers, the US' naval forces are globally superior; the US maintains more than 700 bases worldwide. The US' military predominance is hardly influenced by whether, or to what extent, this enormous US military expenditure is necessary, or reasonable, or whether it has to be regarded as hypertrophic: The US rules the seas, the sky and space.

The annual economic performance of the US, its gross domestic product, amounts to about 21% of the world's total global performance, with only 5% of the world's population, and with a considerable share of this being accounted for by the military sector. At present, this corresponds to almost the total economic output of the EU member states.

The US rules finance: 80% of global stock-exchange turnover is made on Wall Street. The US makes the rules in international accounting, and also uses the threat of potentially huge liability claims in promoting its interests.

The general education level in the US is bad compared to Europe, and we can describe its primary and secondary school sector as being below average. But, nonetheless, the US still has the highest density of renowned universities, whose leadership in science and research is unchallenged. English has become the global language of finance, business and science, the new *lingua franca*. This also applies to the most important scientific publications. The decisive factor is above all the extraordinarily high research budget of the US: The amount of money dedicated to research in the US amounts to nearly half of overall global research expenditure. It is no coincidence that a majority of Nobel Prize winners comes from the US, or works there.

While "God bless America" is part of political everyday life in the US, we are experiencing a creeping secularisation in Europe. Sociologists mainly blame urbanisation, which has made old bonds disappear and has enthroned new gods. These gods reign today in the temples of consumerism and in the churches of distraction (Josef Joffe). But if we compare America to Europe, this explanation is not entirely satisfactory, as America is urbanised to a similar degree as Europe. From an economic point of view, we can find a more plausible explanation. The welfare state in Europe is much wealthier than in the US. Thus state welfare in Europe has taken over the tasks formerly fulfilled by the churches, such as schools, hospitals, poor relief, even spiritual guidance, almost completely.

The US today also dominates the market for consumer culture, from jeans to Coca Cola to McDonald's. In many areas, globalisation seems to carry the label "made in the US". Popular music is predominantly American, and some 80% of the films shown worldwide come from Hollywood. America also claims leadership in western culture, even if this leadership is being challenged internationally.

Europe's Economic Future between the US and the Far East

More fact-oriented arguments, however, represent the US as the predominant power in world trade and on the global financial market – an influential power which does not really benefit the European economy.

America today is the consumer society *par excellence*, it is globally "the consumer of last resort". While European, and even more so Asian, countries are increasing their savings, and while their economies are suffering from weak consumption, Americans are spending money like there was no tomorrow; they hardly save anymore, and instead of building up reserves, accumulate debt. The state incurs debt, not least in order to make war. The typical picture in most countries is that while governments and enterprises accumulate debt, this is matched by the net savings of households. Not so in the US, where private households also live on credit. On the one hand, and in the short term, this is a very successful strategy, since the American economy has impressive growth rates. On the other hand, this consumer behaviour is reflected in a record current account deficit, currently amounting to 600 billion US dollars, or about 6% of gross domestic product.

Financing this current account deficit requires a daily influx of funds to the amount of 2.6 billion dollars. These financial flows come mainly from states in the Far East and their central banks, above all Japan and China. The US absorbs about 80% of global annual savings. In the meantime the US has turned from being the biggest creditor to being the biggest debtor country; its foreign debt has reached a record high of 2.5 trillion dollars (or 25% of its own annual economic output). This situation undoubtedly puts the omnipotence of the US into question because it makes the US prone to being blackmailed financially, and vulnerable to a different kind of terror, namely potential financial terror.

Countries in the Far East are accumulating export surpluses and dollar foreign exchange reserves. They have pegged their currencies to the weak dollar so that, with the passage of time, they are grossly undervalued. Due to this pegging arrangement, a depreciating dollar cannot help restore balance in the US. And, the stronger European currencies leave many producers in hopelessly uncompetitive situations. Europe is in danger of sliding downhill along the global economic subsidence slope.

The profound exchange rate misalignments are particularly serious for Europe. While the US, with its high current account deficits and huge budget deficits, is living rakishly beyond its means, the currencies pegged to the dollar, above all the Chinese yuan, are becoming increasingly undervalued. The euro in turn is in the alignment trap. This may be desirable for people travelling abroad, and also proves to be favourable for imports, oil imports for instance. European exports, however, are losing competitiveness. Attempts to compete all but eliminate profitability. The reason is that the production costs are incurred in euro, whereas the revenue is earned in US dollars. Thus, a threat to Europe arises not only from US competition, but increasingly also from the states in the Far East whose currencies are pegged to the dollar. Jammed in between these dollar giants, economic development in Europe is in danger of stagnating while it is gaining momentum in the Far East.

When we take these unfavourable exchange-rate conditions into account, the European economy is subject to threefold pressure. Firstly, the weak dollar puts pressure on exports to the dollar countries, as already mentioned, and on competitiveness. Secondly, Europe's businesses are subject to internal cost pressure due to comparatively high infrastructure prices, for instance for electricity, water, administration, road pricing etc. And thirdly, they are under increasing pressure on output prices, which are then passed on to affect, and destroy, the margins of the producers and suppliers of intermediate goods. This jeopardises supply security in the long run.

With a considerable savings rate of 10%, the European states together are caught in a deflationary environment. In spite of, or, rather, because of, the drive for efficiency gains to cut costs, there is also a gap in demand to be bridged. It is not without reason that one of the first Nobel Prize winners for economics, Paul Samuelson, pointed out that Our Lord had given the economists two eyes, one for supply and the other for demand. Of course, endeavours have to be made to keep the danger of inflation thus provoked at bay, but that is not the most serious of Europe's problems. Currently our biggest problem is weak economic growth.

The US is having its prosperity financed by the rest of the world, and also by Europe. This unjust distribution must not persist in the long run. An all-too abrupt change, however, would result in a serious worldwide recession. Therefore multilateral, and coordinated, adjustments at the level of the most important global players are urgently required.

Currency Supremacy: The Petro-Dollar

World events are now dominated by the United States. This dominance is based on economic and military might, on political influence and pressure as well as on geo-strategic control. In addition, the role of the US dollar as the global reserve currency, most recently represented by the petro-dollar whereby many raw materials were priced in US dollars on global markets, is a further important pillar of US dominance. However, this apparent supremacy is not without its fragility, or "feet of clay" as it were; it is very much dependent on US access to, and guaranteed supplies of, essential raw materials.

We must consider that the US invasion of Iraq in 2003 and the toppling of its former ally, Saddam Hussein, were not solely motivated by political, ideological or even humanitarian considerations. Nor was the security of oil supplies a dominant consideration. Many American journalists are now convinced that the overriding motive behind this military misadventure was a perceived need to bolster the importance of the dollar against encroachments by the new euro currency. In November 2000, Saddam Hussein had announced his intention to invoice future oil deliveries in euro instead of dollars. The United States viewed this as an obvious threat to the supremacy of the dollar which, in turn, carried a clear challenge to the influence of America on the world oil market; in addition, it contained a perceived threat to the economy of the United States.

The reserve-currency role of the dollar, bolstered by the petro-dollar, enables the United States to finance its external deficits with its own fiat, or paper, currency. As the only country on Earth entitled to "print" dollars and issue dollar securities, it can benefit uniquely from the global demand for dollars arising from the reserve-currency role of its currency. Taking a narrow view of the situation, one can imagine the USA printing dollars and satisfying the world demand for the currency in exchange for goods and services – as close to a Garden of Eden existence as we are ever likely to get!

This cannot continue indefinitely, and the exploitation of this situation contains the seeds of its own destruction – somewhat like killing the goose that laid golden eggs. But it does have a short-term monopolistic "seigniorage" benefit which may appear very attractive to politicians with a short planning horizon. And, in the longer term, the resultant profusion of dollar securities, or debts, tends to sustain US financial securities markets where size exerts a positive network effect.

This privileged situation was seriously threatened by the introduction of the euro as a rival and the risk of the emergence of a "petro-euro". The establishment of an Asiatic Currency Unit (ACU) carries precisely the same threat. The "mountain of debt" created not only by the government of the United States but, rather exceptionally, by American households as well, poses a dual risk; the United States may be exposed to the risk of financial blackmail if it genuinely tries to honour its debts, and to the risk of being relegated to the ranks of a third-world power if it doesn't.

In either event, the risk of a serious and protracted recession in the United States is not something which even that country's most vociferous critics can look forward to with any degree of smug satisfaction. For this reason, the problem is not one to be resolved unilaterally by the USA alone, but will require a concerted multilateral effort. The alternative, an economic "Armageddon", is not something which can be looked forward to with relish.

Imbalances in the Global Economy

Trans-continental trade flows are a further example of how economic framework conditions have changed to the disadvantage of Europe in the course of the geopolitical and geo-strategic revolutions. Until recently, the volume of US trade relations with Europe and with Asia were approximately the same, while today Asia is already 50% ahead, and soon will be close to 100%.

Similar to Japan in the 1950s and 1960s, China has also reported strong economic growth since the late 1970s; its real growth rate could reach 10% p.a. in the next few years. China has long been respected as a world power in Asia. Even though the boom in China's economy can be compared to the previous booms in Japan or South Korea, we have to take into account that China currently has ten times as many inhabitants as Japan, and thirty times as many as South Korea. Japan has been an economic power for quite some time and is now also increasing its military potential. Still, due to its self-imposed political isolation, it seems unlikely that Japan will become a global political and military power, in addition to its global economic and financial influence.

Russia remains an important factor in global policy due to its huge territory, its richness in natural resources and energy reserves, and, last but not least, because it is a nuclear power. Russia is partly dependent on international help for successfully implementing political and economic reforms, not least because it has still to overcome its internal structural problems.

The Market Economy: Half of the World's Population Returns Home

As early as at the beginning of the last century, John Hay, then US foreign secretary, astutely remarked that the Mediterranean was the ocean of the past, the Atlantic the ocean of the present, and the Pacific the ocean of the future.

The division of the world into two camps was characterised by the Western market economies on the one hand, while on the other, we had the trio of Russia undergoing Stalinist isolation, China hermetically sealed off under the leadership of Mao Zedong and India pursuing the autarkic economic goals of Pandit Nehru, the first post-independence prime minister of the sub-continent. Once these systems were seen to have outlived their purpose, a good half of the world's population adopted once more the market-based economic system and, thereby, returned to the world's political stage.

A preview of the likely economic development of the next 15 years reveals the following: The world economy in 2020 A.D. will be about two thirds larger than in 2005, providing the 3.5% average growth rate of GDP experienced in the past 25 years continues into the future. The shares of individual counties in this global GDP will be sharply redistributed in favour of the growing Asian markets. The real incomes enjoyed in the USA and Europe will grow much more slowly.

The growth and the strength of the Asian economy are even more impressive when one extends the time-horizon under observation. In the 15th century, the highly developed countries of India and China together accounted for about 75% of world output; between 1500 and 1800 A.D., these two countries still accounted for about half of world output, whereas this ratio had fallen to 8.7% by 1950. Today their share of global economic performance is estimated at about 20% and this is expected to increase to 30% in the coming 15 years. According to some very optimistic projections, their share could rise to 45% by the year 2050.

The economic miracle experienced by these two countries, which some commentators fuse together under the name "Chindia", is triggering concern if not actual fear in some quarters; even George W. Bush has sometimes joined this chorus. The reality is that the emergence and progress of these countries is much less a cause for fear and anxiety than the alternative scenario, that "Chindia" might become a region of stagnation and adversity.

By the year 2020, the GDP of China alone is projected to overtake that of either the USA or Europe. India is also on the verge of overtaking the European economy in real terms. With an average annual real growth rate of 5% in the coming 15 years, the real incomes of Asian households will be amongst the fastest growing in the world. Nevertheless, it will be much too soon to think in terms of an "Asian century", no matter how much the Chinese government might like to think in those terms. As soon as we look at the statistics in *per capita* terms, it becomes immediately apparent that these countries are still developing and emerging economies and will remain so for quite some time to come.

Rising Powers: China and India

The historic "old" countries with their ancient cultures and their exploding mass populations have returned to the world stage, with China and India leading the way. Both countries have civilisations which are several millennia old; they are the most populous countries and together are home to two fifths of the world's population. Currently, China's population is still the larger of the two, but in about 20 years' time, India will have overtaken China and will have become the most populous state in the world. Politically, India is currently also the largest democratic state on our planet, even though it is a complicated democracy. China is governed by a communist, single-party regime that has been in power since 1945; currently it is experiencing its fifth set of leaders. In the early 1980s, under the leadership of Deng Xiao Ping, China opened up to globalisation and became market-oriented and liberal in more and more areas. In India, this opening-up process started later, in 1991, under former finance minister and current head of government, Singh. India is also progressing comparatively more slowly.

Amongst other things, this explains the impressive economic momentum and high growth rates in China. China's gross domestic product today amounts to approximately two and a half times the GDP of India. Led by the US and followed by Germany and Japan, China is now the fourth-largest country in terms of exports, with a considerable trade surplus, especially vis-à-vis the US. Accordingly, its currency reserves have now increased to more than 600 billion US dollars, whereas India's reserves amount to 135 billion US dollars. Foreign direct investment has contributed considerably to this prosperity. Associated with this foreign investment, there has also been an enormous technology transfer and exchange of know-how. In China, foreign investment since 1980 has reached a total of 500 billion US dollars; in India, it amounts to about 130 billion US dollars. In the year 2004 alone, 60 billion US dollars flowed into China, whereas India's share was a comparatively modest 5 billion dollars. Very soon, China and India will grow into heavyweights in global economy and global political terms, in spite of internal political problems or the dangers which such rapid growth can entail (as can be seen from the example of Japan). Sooner or later, Russia and Brazil will also join the group of the superpowers. Indonesia, with about 200 million inhabitants the Islamic state with the largest population in the world, is also about to cross the threshold.

A Global Struggle for Resources

The age of petroleum, natural gas, and even of water, has become an era of concern about supply. The sharp price increases of recent years have left no one unaffected, from large multinational corporations to the private end-user, and carry a clear message of impending shortages.

Even today we can see clearly to what extent aspiring economic powers absorb raw materials and energy resources worldwide. Thirst for oil and hunger for raw materials have led to global competition with regard to these fundamental economic goods. Increasing prices already provide evidence for this development, and even more considerable increases in prices are to be expected. Within a few years prices have risen drastically: the price of oil two and a half times, the price of steel threefold, and the price of coal has even soared to five times its former level.

Petroleum is sometimes described as the "life blood of civilisation", the fuel of the world economy. Others depict it as the "devil's tears". Potential output is expected to reach its peak in the next five years and to level off, or plateau, thereafter. Demand, on the other hand, is expected to continue rising, thus giving rise to a growing output gap. The same scenario applies to natural gas, although with a time-lag.

In the context of the world economy, the strategic importance of petroleum oil and natural gas cannot be overstated. This makes it very likely that they will be at the core of future conflicts. That China has already advanced to become the second largest consumer of petroleum behind the United States gives rise to a future scenario whereby Washington and Beijing are depicted as two super tankers set on a long-term collision course. Once more, one must realise that future developments are likely to be heavily influenced by the fact that half of the world's known reserves of petroleum are geographically located in politically unstable regions, Saudi Arabia and the Persian Gulf.

Apart from the superpower the USA, other countries also have a good chance of becoming future "global players" in the international power game, not least because of their industrial might, their importance as consumer markets or their near self-sufficiency in raw materials. Such countries would include the old, and new, superpowers of Japan, China and India. "Old" Europe can also be included in this elite group. Russia must also feature prominently on the world geo-economic map because of its size as well as its enormous resources of certain raw materials. And Brazil can also be considered to face an unencumbered energy future.

The strategy for economic survival and success under this increasingly threatening cost pressure can be found in the field of innovation and research. It will only be possible to cope with increasing raw material and oil prices if, in return, procedures can be found that replace traditional fuels, and if alternative products are developed that require fewer material inputs.

The greatest deficits of Europe vis-à-vis the states of the Far East probably lie in Europe's lack of innovative power and in the fact that the states neglect these important investments in the future. Europe's self-satisfied stagnation and the specifically European resistance to vested rights are in crass contrast to Asia's momentum and its overwhelming will to succeed. Europe seems to have already lost the race mentioned earlier: A phrase well known from boxing says "the best fighters are hungry fighters", and, in contrast to Asia, Europe is not a hungry fighter.

Lang Lang, the world-famous young pianist, characterised the differences between the Western world and his native China, by referring to this mentality and to everyday life. In an interview he said that he had met many people full of energy and with a lot of potential in Europe, striving for a good life. But they did not realise that in order to achieve it, they would have to have a dream, a goal in life that they head for as directly as possible and with as much discipline as possible.

Will the "American Dream" become a Global Nightmare?

The world sees the American way of life and the American Dream as having lost some of their splendour, not least because of a particular missionary spirit with which these ideals have been disseminated by the Bush administration in particular. In his inauguration speech for his second term in office, George W. Bush invoked the word "freedom" 49 times, referring to a Hobbesian freedom, of course, intended to justify fighting and war.

Many realities created by the American Dream meet with rejection and criticism particularly in Europe. The low turnout in US elections, at less than 47% and lower than in 15 European states by comparison, casts doubt on the noble ideals of democracy. The quality of public services has fallen far behind those of the EU average or Canada. Career opportunities in the US are often praised for being boundless, classless and without prejudice, with biographies from Henry Kissinger to Madeleine Albright, from Bill Gates to Arnold Schwarzenegger as shining examples. In reality, there is an increasing divide between the rich and the poor, and the much-vaunted opportunities are vanishing, as witnessed by manifestly deteriorating income and employment opportunities. In the land of the American Dream, social security does not play a role comparable to European standards.

A high crime rate, the largest number of prison inmates in the world on a *per capita* basis, and adherence to the death penalty tarnish the image of this paradise, the dream image of an "illuminated city on the hill". Europeans are often alienated by the American legal system which produces such effects, since this system is clearly also an expression of the Hobbesian approach to conflict resolution already mentioned: There are 350 lawyers to every 100,000 inhabitants in the US, but only 150 in Germany, and a mere 16 in Japan.

The main point of criticism, however, is that the US often approaches global problems with too much self-confidence, and increasingly with self-righteousness, even arrogance. High energy consumption in the US is taking its toll: Having rejected the Kyoto Protocol, the United States is still the front-runner in producing global CO_2 damage. Five percent of the world's population consume 25% of global oil production, more than half of which has to be imported. The US is therefore dependent on energy and energy imports to a large extent. Despite the fact that the "oil age" is probably already past its peak, crude oil as an energy source will probably continue to be important in the US for a long time to come. This dependence on energy is often blamed for the geo-strategic behaviour of the US, to the point of engaging in a policy of "blood for oil".

Europe's Role in the "American Century"

In view of the determination of the Bush administration to go to war with Iraq, Susan Sontag, the famous cultural sociologist who died in late 2004, became a gloomy hortative Cassandra, forecasting the dawning of a global American dictatorship. Even though her prophecy is drastically and provokingly exaggerated, it provides an image of the discomfort Europe thinks it has to feel when dealing with the US. Globally speaking, the US is increasingly pursuing a unilateral policy which today – in contrast to former times and in contrast to its own traditions and legal concepts – no longer attaches any obvious importance to legitimacy. Thus, however, we can see the fatal flaw in a policy which refuses even to allow for the possibility of error (George Soros). In the sense of the Martian-martial and Hobbesian ideology, with superior forces you can win wars, but you cannot win lasting peace. Even the uni-polar hyper-power has its limitations because, faced with global problems, global cooperation and international collaboration are indispensable.

The American sociologist, Daniel Bell stated a few decades ago that any nation state is too small for big problems and at the same time too big for small problems. Tony Blair recently put it in a nutshell when he related this insight to the current situation and explained that no state could solve the big problems of the world, with terrorism among them, on its own, however powerful it may be. Not even a "special relationship" such as that linking the United Kingdom and the US would be up to solving these big global problems (as demonstrated by the Iraq War).

"Soft Power" as Europe's Strength

The most recent military misadventures of the US in Afghanistan and in Iraq have shown clearly how quickly the biggest military power in the world can win wars, but how ineffectual it is, by contrast, in attempting to pacify a country. Without the support of the international community of states, the restoration of peace and normality will be difficult to achieve, as was dramatically illustrated by the American war against terrorism. A *war* against terrorism – it could have been better and more appropriately called a "fight against terrorism" – cannot even be waged, let alone be won, by America alone. The *fight* against terrorism with global alliances is much more promising. In this context, it will also become evident that "soft power" is maybe more important and more efficient than "hard power" (Joseph

S. Nye). Weapons are not the appropriate means, or at any rate never the ultimate means, of solving conflicts.

The world's danger and conflict spots can certainly not be defused by military means. On the contrary, intelligent "soft power", serving peaceful prevention via the elimination of injustices, is required here to a great extent. The task is not only to fight the consequences, but more importantly the causes of these conflicts. International law will also have to be amended to this objective.

As opposed to centuries past, when war still was the great arbitrator, the most interesting types of power today no longer come out of the barrel of a gun. Today there is much more to be gained by getting others to want what you want yourself, and that has something to do with cultural attraction, with ideology, with opinion leadership, and with the chances of benefiting from cooperation. This is how Joseph Joffe characterised the forward-looking potential of "soft power".

In the Islamic world, the US and Europe today are confronted in equal measure with backwardness, lack of development, deficits in democracy, and a large number of regions of political unrest. The Islamic world covers the area from Mindanao to Marrakesh, is home to 1.3 billion people, and holds the largest part of the global oil reserves. The alliance of the "free western world" is called upon to help the Islamic world to cross the threshold into the 21st century, in the same way that the Arabian influence was once important for the period of prosperity of Medieval culture in the occident.

Ex oriente fiat lux: EU Accession Perspectives for Turkey

Last but not least the possible and desirable integration of Turkey into the EU has to be regarded as consistently continuing this tradition of mutual cultural stimulation spanning several millennia.

Despite all the difficulties still to be overcome, the cultural, spiritual and historic links that already exist between

Europe and Turkey, where we can find the fertile soil of antique and Christian and thus occidental history, seem to be an expandable foundation on which to build a future partnership. The issue of Turkey's EU membership, discussed with absurd emotionality, once again raises the question of how the European Union sees itself and how it defines itself. But even if you are traditionally minded and base European identity on a "Europe of Cathedrals" (Robert Schuman), i.e. on Christianity, you could still argue that in this respect Turkey also was one of the cradles of Europe.

Turkey's culture and history have been closely linked with those of Europe for a long time, and Turkey's development over the last one hundred years documents an even further convergence convincingly. The secular Republic of Turkey founded on 29 October 1923 by Kemal Atatürk is strongly oriented towards Europe, and the reforms, the pace of which fortunately has accelerated over the past few years, are also oriented towards the EU. A residual problem, however, is that the elite's orientation towards the west has caused tensions within the Muslim population, and that Turkey still has shortcomings with regard to minority rights and women's rights.

Populist xenophobes within the EU scent an over-expansion of the Union if Turkey accedes, and thus see the deepening of European integration in danger. But beyond these anxieties, the more important challenges lie in the necessary structural adaptations of the EU. The fear that Turkey, which would have the largest national population in the EU, would soon become the key factor in EU policy, has to be counteracted tactically in foreign, economic and financial policy, not least also by defining welfare-state criteria.

It has to be considered, however, that the EU with Turkey as a full member would extend beyond the Black Sea and Anatolia towards the Middle East, and would thus also undoubtedly give up the safe distance between Europe and regions of political unrest, whose conflict potential today is beyond the actual possibilities of Europe to cope. But the contrary opinion also has something going for it: Some political decisions, in particular in foreign and defence policy, would be easier for Europe to take with Turkey than they are without Turkey. In any case, Europe, with its increasing share of an Islamic population, has a far more vital interest in a peaceful, prosperous and democratic Middle East than the US.

If the preconditions within Turkey itself have been fulfilled and if the EU has established its own absorption capacity, Turkey's EU membership is to be supported. After all, the "Copenhagen Criteria" of 1993 – one of the most important documents in the history of the EU – have formulated clear guidelines on the conditions for the accession of new members. Up to now, these criteria have not been fulfilled by Turkey, so it will hardly be possible for Turkey to accede before 2015.

Questions of Identity: Where are the Boundaries of Europe?

There are challenges for the European Union today that are much closer geographically and much more topical, i.e. the integration of, and how to deal with, the Balkan states and the Ukraine. The Ukraine is not only important for Europe because of its oil pipe-lines; it also constitutes a promising and important challenge, since it could become the bridge for the democratisation of, and closer links with, Russia (Zbigniew Brzezinski). The Ukrainian population has already emphatically demonstrated its genuine commitment to democracy and national independence, but it would now require European help and encouragement in order to consolidate and continue the process that has been started.

Henry Kissinger had already hinted in conversations at the parallels between the Ukraine and Mexico, stating that what Mexico was for the US, the Ukraine was for Russia. However, former Hungarian deputy prime minister Jozsef Marjai, a recognised expert of those political zones which suffered for a long time under Soviet rule and communist dictatorship, also pointed out the following difference: Many Mexicans live in the US, but few US-Americans live in Mexico; many Russians live in Ukraine, but hardly any Ukrainians live in Russia.

Not least with a view to a European-Russian partnership, the Ukraine's accession to a larger European community should gradually provide a good argument for an open, welcoming and flexible way for Europe to deal with nations which are willing to join.

Due to Austria's geographic proximity to the Balkans as well as to the former "East Bloc", these issues are particularly relevant and would provide a challenge for Austria to show appropriate commitment. However, there is no such commitment to be seen at the moment, if we look at how much conflict there is in the way Austria is dealing with its immediate neighbouring countries, as if it were even actively looking for conflicts. This has been shown amongst others by the issues of the Benes Decrees, Temelin, Bohunice and Mohovce. At the same time, Austria has also failed to create an appropriate transport infrastructure facilitating trade, for instance, with the Czech Republic.

Austria has failed to assume the role of an advocate within the EU in favour of further steps to integrate its eastern neighbours, despite the fact that these steps are in Austria's own political and economic interest. Neither does Austria support the countries of the Balkans in its vicinity in their democratic maturing process and in their wish for European integration. The European aspirations of the Ukraine or Moldavia, for instance, go completely unmentioned in Austria.

EU-topia and the European Dream

Against the backdrop of scepticism towards the American Dream, you would now expect the concept of a European Dream to develop; however, the continent has only just about succeeded in developing into a European Union. When assessing the opportunities Europe can avail itself of, together with America, in a global context, a key question arises: Can the EU develop a sufficient degree of political commitment, beyond socio-cultural coherence, to be able to take a common position on a long list of questions on global issues? Or, will it remain a group of countries with limited influence, acting nationally with strongly diverging positions in foreign policy?

It is typical that, as already mentioned in the context of the discussion about enlargement, even the leading thinkers of European integration disagree on the limits and opportunities of this entity called Europe. Some may regard Europe as a mere mind game geared towards a prospering internal market, an arrangement without any political importance, and consequently regard the common currency as rounding off the common market rather than being the starting point of a political union (Ralf Dahrendorf).

But no matter how anybody may assess the future perspectives of the European Union, he or she cannot but recognise the progress already made. This voluntary association of sovereign states has no precedent and no model in history. It can demonstrate in an exemplary manner how different states, despite their diversity, can cooperate effectively under the premises of a liberal order and a pluralistic system. The EU is a cooperation model for even greater regions, and what has been remarkably successfully implemented in its currently 27 member states, could one day become a blueprint in a much larger context, namely in an ideal "one world".

Where Europe Stands and Where It Wants to Go

Today's reality, however, confronts us with other tasks. Through growing economic integration, through the monetary union of today's 13 euro countries, and eventually through implemented EU enlargement, Europe has become a giant whose economic performance even exceeds that of the US. Politically, however, Europe has remained a midget, and from a military point of view, it is a newt.

Geopolitical and geo-economic revolutions notwithstanding, Europe's thinking is still caught up in provincial nation-state illusions of sovereignty. In the global context, Europe can only gain influence if it pools its resources skilfully, and if it brings itself to having a common foreign, security and economic policy. Europe has to promote its integration further; the common market and monetary union have to be merged into a common economic policy. And Europe has to learn to speak with one voice. Helmut Schmidt, a staunch supporter of European integration motivated by a "strategic and patriotic interest", deduces the "principle of self-assertion through community" for Europe from the geopolitical constellations of the 21st century.

We need a European Dream as a response and as an alternative to the American Dream. For this dream, we most of all require a European awareness, a European public, and European media. It would be up to the media as well as politics to develop a European public. The media in Europe are mostly nationally oriented, so that, typically enough, the only truly "European" newspaper is the American "Herald Tribune". The political deficit mainly consists of the fact that, in terms of public opinion, the national members of parliament still have a much stronger legitimacy bonus than the Members of the European Parliament. The low turnout in European parliamentary elections, and even the election campaigns themselves, which are mostly of a nationalist populist character, are sad indicators of the lack of awareness of the importance of the European Parliament. Without a European *demos*, there will never be a European democracy.

During the past century, the world's population quadrupled, and since the mid-20th century it has doubled; it is likely to continue to grow rapidly from over 6 billion to 9 billion people. Due to revolutionary developments in transport and in telecommunications, the global economy has "intertwined" even further, as Kurt Tucholsky (a German writer and journalist in the first half of the 20th century) already said in an ironic aphorism. This process of globalisation goes hand in hand with great opportunities, but naturally it is not devoid of risks and dangers either. International co-operation is required to limit these risks and dangers; building national or continental fortresses can certainly not provide a solution.

On the occasion of the signing of the Treaty of Rome, the New York Times published a commentary on the European integration process on 26 March 1957, which contained sentiments which are equally valid today, even if Europeans have never really taken them to heart. "Behind this development is a constantly growing wish for the unification of Europe, as the only real possibility of restoring the continent to its former position of power, enabling it to survive in peace ... All these intentions are born in the realisation that the European nation states have become a historical anachronism, and are no longer capable of preserving their independence on their own. For this reason, they have no choice but to unite – or go under."

The Future of the Transatlantic Community

In 2007, the European Union celebrated the 50th anniversary of the signing of the Treaty of Rome, confident in the fact that the initial six member states had meanwhile grown to twenty seven. The process of European integration is older than that, however, and amounts to 55 years if we include the so-called *Montanunion*, as the Coal and Steel Community was known. And, it is sixty years since President Truman expounded his Truman Doctrine before Congress in March 1947, which drew a sharp distinction between freedom and totalitarianism, and which became the basis for Marshal Aid and the regeneration of post-war Europe.

The combined result is that Europe has meanwhile enjoyed three generations of peace, security and growing prosperity. The positive effects were particularly obvious during the "cold war", which for Europe amounted to a "cold peace", thanks to the protective shield offered by the United States and NATO. It is important that we show our appreciation for the assistance of the United States, which rescued us from even worse consequences of our own folly through its interventions in two World Wars. And we should not lose sight of this debt of gratitude merely because the behaviour of the current neo-conservative political elite in the USA is engendering a powerful sentiment of anti-Americanism.

It will also be necessary to reshape the transatlantic community, given the necessity of global cooperation, since each individual state is too small for the big problems confronting it. The Europeans will be called upon to overcome their distrust and anti-Americanism, and to become aware once again how vital a strong America is, particularly for Europe. And Americans will be called upon to cultivate a healthy self-confidence and an ability to accept criticism. In this way, America can build up a reservoir of trust which the US can benefit from when, in individual cases, it is necessary to act unilaterally (Robert Kagan).

This transatlantic community is as necessary for Europe as it is for the US, in order to cope jointly with common challenges, such as the Ukraine or Turkey, the Middle East, or Iran, and in seeking global peace. Madeleine Albright, being an American and a European, also says that America is an indispensable nation at any rate.

What Europe Can Learn and Must Learn

Since the end of the Second World War, the population of the US has doubled to 300 million people, and will increase to 400 million in the near future. Due to the low birth rate, the European population will stagnate and may even decrease in future, a fate also expected to be shared by Austria. The question of Turkey's EU membership will also have to be considered against this background, by the way.

The ageing society raises many issues, and not only how to finance retirement pensions. We therefore need an intelligent immigration policy; in individual cases it may even be necessary to advertise for selective immigration. Contrary to prejudiced opinions, migration also has a tradition in Europe, albeit certainly in forms and dimensions different from migration in America.

There is also another aspect in which a future-oriented Europe would do well to adapt to the American model. Despite the fact that the European states have better general education systems, their university and research sectors are clearly inferior to those in the US. I have already pointed out the correlation between the budgets and the qualities of top American universities, and the same correlation applies to research expenditure: The US makes 100 billion dollars more available for research and development annually than the old continent dedicates to these important future-oriented tasks.

The PISA study and the development of the labour market make it more and more evident that the European education systems, and thus also the Austrian education system, require extensive reforms. There is still a shortage of schools and kindergartens that are open all day; again and again deficits are found with regard to qualified teachers, up to headmaster level; and the political weighting of education expenditure sometimes borders on the absurd. Silvio Borner, an economist from Basle, showed, for instance, that in Switzerland, the cost of the education of a primary school pupil is roughly equivalent to that of keeping three cows. For all intents and purposes, this comparison is also representative of the European Union which spends half of its total budget on agriculture.

When education is completed, this issue is directly transferred to the labour market, which no longer offers sufficient employment opportunities to first-time job seekers, even the well-educated.

In the year 2000, the EU set itself the ambitious target of becoming the most dynamic and competitive knowledge-based economy in the world, by means of the so-called Lisbon Process. The mid-term review of this process, however, is extremely sobering if we look at how far Europe's growth lags behind that of the US and the growth of the rising countries in the Far East. By 2010, the European Union plans to allocate three percent of its gross domestic product to research and development. In order to be able to achieve this objective, R&D expenditure will have to increase by eight percent annually, and an additional 700,000 researchers and scientists will be required.

Scarcity of resources and other global threats can produce tidal waves in the global political amphitheatre. Each state of the EU-27 is individually too small to dare face the buffeting of the waves of world politics and the storms of the world economy completely alone. It is only together that the European states can be regarded as seaworthy in a global storm. Only together can Europe be regarded as a player in the international political game, and not simply the political football. The world needs a strong Europe, and one which is capable of living up to, and accepting, its global responsibilities. Only thus can we hope to witness a "single world" which presents a multi-polar and democratic global economy.

And Where Does Austria Stand?

Despite the fact that it has been an EU member for ten years, Austria has not become more open, more urbane or more dynamic, in contrast with what we might have expected or at least have wished for. It seems as if this country wanted to remain stuck and unchanged as an "island of the blessed". Journalist Margaretha Kopeinig formulated this view even more drastically when she said that Austrians seemed to have stopped on the assembly line of time.

The competitiveness and attractiveness of Europe as a business location keep deteriorating, since there is no coordinated common economic policy. In the meantime, the euro has become much too strong, the interest rate level has been too high for a long time, and the same applies to the tax burden. As a consequence, Europe has little economic momentum, smaller increases in productivity, and its growth is increasingly falling behind, despite the fact that the EU countries have a relatively high savings rate of 10% on average (as opposed to less than 1% in the US). There are no reasonable plans with regard to financial policy or economic policy as to what should happen to these savings. This worrying situation manifests itself in an unemployment rate that is already high and still rising, as well as in the financing problems of state budgets.

The energy of the European administration seems to lose itself in a sea of regulations which would be a credit to the well-known Kakanian-Austrian preoccupation with bureaucracy (the Austro-Hungarian Monarchy was called the "k&k" monarchy, deriving from "*kaiserlich & königlich*" – imperial and royal, since its emperor was Emperor of Austria and King of Hungary. It was infamous for its exaggerated bureaucracy and overregulation, and in literature became known as "*Kakanien*", the term being invented by Robert Musil). Both at national and at European level, the number of asphyxiating regulations is increasing, and most restrict economic fields of activity excessively. The Federal state, the Federal provinces and the Union should eventually follow the requirement of Montesquieu, the legal philosopher with the broad vision – 2005 was "Montesquieu year" – "If it is not necessary to make a law, then it is necessary not to make a law."

What Europe requires urgently is a growth initiative consisting of investment in future-oriented areas such as education, research and innovation, as well as a modern infrastructure, and considerably fewer regulations. Their motto should be "as much market as possible, as much state as necessary". Correspondingly this also has to apply to the social security net where people must exercise their own initiative in providing for their old age, and take responsibility for their own lives; otherwise the social welfare net will tear because it can no longer be financed.

However, in order not to advocate pure neo-liberalism, or even to advise the state to use subterfuges in transferring its responsibilities to others, we have to insist that a market economy should be as efficient, social and ecological as possible; otherwise it is neither legitimate nor desirable.

Leaving aside the popular excuse that the culprits are presumably to be found in the regulations jungle of Brussels, this statement in favour of a modernisation and growth initiative applies with special force to Austria.

The Austrian anniversary year 2005 was an occasion on which to remember that the last 60 years, but above all the last 50 years of the Second Republic, tell a success story. This success story shows – and I hope I have been able to support this argument – the close connection between the economy and politics, or the direct impact of economic policy on social developments. Austrian trade union leaders of the calibre of Anton Benya or Johann Böhm also knew that a satisfactory social policy has to be based on a sound economic policy.

Fifty years ago (and that is an anniversary, too), Ludwig Erhard remarked that "Only on the basis of a healthy economy can society achieve its true goals." In contrast with this insight, public thinking in Austria is very hostile to economy and technology.

The circumstances in 1945, by comparison, were more favourable to a young Austrian state than those of the First Republic after the First World War. That Austria was able to capitalise on these favourable conditions is proved not least by the fact that Austria managed to negotiate the State Treaty. The direct result of this treaty was that the Republic of Austria left the period of occupation behind and was released into freedom. Neutrality status was required for the State Treaty, and neutrality was a highly important instrument during the Cold War. Today, Austrian neutrality has lost this importance, which is why it should not be used as an excuse for not having to take a position or not to act within Europe while at the same time being a full member of the EU and the euro zone.

Missed Opportunities and New Perspectives

It is also thanks to the neutrality bonus that during the period of the Cold War Austria enjoyed a good international reputation as a location for high-level meetings and negotiations. Since 1957, Vienna has been the headquarters of the International Atomic Energy Agency and is the third UN headquarters after New York and Geneva; since 1967, it has also hosted the headquarters of UNIDO. In June 1961, the legendary meeting between John F. Kennedy and Nikita Khrushchev took place in Vienna. In 1979, Jimmy Carter and Leonid Brezhnev signed the SALT II Agreement on limiting strategic nuclear weapons in this city. After the end of the Cold War, Vienna's importance decreased noticeably, despite its hosting the OSCE Secretariat, and the demand for Austria's role as a mediator went into decline. The reason for this loss of importance is to be found above all in the fact that after the Cold War, Austria missed the opportunity of giving itself and its role as a mediator a new profile, since neutrality was, and is, no longer a factor in international politics. Austria is lacking too much both in political courage to take a stance, and in well-educated, far-sighted politicians of global stature in foreign policy. Personalities such as former chancellor Bruno Kreisky, who gained his international reputation when he acted as a mediator in the conflict in the Middle East, should not be a matter of the past forever.

Today, Austria could use the Scandinavian countries as a model, to which Vienna has yielded its former importance as a mediator. Norway also celebrated an anniversary recently, namely the 100th anniversary of its foundation as a nation state, and presents itself internationally as a nation of peace. It has rendered outstanding services to other countries when acting as a mediator and arbitrator in disputes involving countries such as Haiti, Sri Lanka, Burma, Columbia, Pakistan, the Philippines, Eritrea, Sudan and continuously also the Middle East.

As a result of successful reconstruction after the Second World War, Austria has been able to catch up and become one of the richest countries in the world, largely thanks to the US Marshal Plan and membership of the European Union. Until the dissolution of the East Bloc, Austria was precariously close to the Iron Curtain, on the edge of the western world. It became obvious that you don't have to be located at the heart of Europe in order to have Europe in your heart. Today Austria has returned to the heart of Europe, and through EU enlargement towards the east is once more renewing its ties with the Danube region, so familiar from its historical past.

Our external payments balances, both on merchandise trade and on current account, serve to show how effectively the Austrian economy has grasped the opportunities which were presented. Unfortunately, we have not shown the same positive approach on the political front; quite the opposite, our political relations towards our neighbours have been characterised by bickering, as can be seen from our short-sighted response to the transit-traffic and atomic-energy issues and our inhospitable approach to immigration. It is nothing short of a disgrace that Austria has hardly done anything to improve and modernise European traffic links in the period since the gentle revolution of 1989.

What Europe requires is also necessary in Austria: We need European awareness instead of anti-Americanism in order to organise our transatlantic relations wisely. We need European commitment instead of euroscepticism and EU rejection, and we need a reasonable immigration policy instead of xenophobic defence against immigration.

The European, and therefore also Austrian, recipe for success contains the "four Is": promoting Initiative, Innovation, Investment in non-monetary capital and human capital, and Infrastructure. For the last of those, you may confidently believe an old proverb from the aspiring economic power China which says, "If you want to be rich, you have to build roads".

For the success of a European economic policy, we have to create the best possible infrastructure, adequate framework conditions in commercial law, but above all we have to limit the explosion of bureaucratic regulations in a reasonable manner. We need an active European monetary policy and a future-oriented education and funding policy in order to survive in a global environment.

Within the EU, Austria itself, like all small countries, has to fulfil a constructive role in interacting with its neighbours. Austria accounts for about 1.8% of the population of the entire European Union; it constitutes about 2% of the landmass of the EU and produces about 2.2% of total output. Austria can contribute to the achievement of our communal goals only insofar as we quickly and enthusiastically put our own house in order with regard to economic policy, deregulation, provision of infrastructure, and adequate funding of education and research. Only then can we be regarded as mature Europeans. It is a daunting task and a major challenge, but we owe it to future generations to make the effort.

Austria Above All, If Only She Is Willing

Much remains to be done in order to position Austria in the global networks and make it fit for the challenges of an American century also in future. Conscious of our own identity, we Austrians have to learn quickly to act as Europeans in order to be able to live as global citizens.

"Österreich über alles, wann es nur will" ("Austria Above All, If Only She Is Willing") is the title of a book by Philipp Wilhelm von Hörnigk, who immigrated to Austria from Frankfurt. It appeared in 1684, one year after the Second Turkish Siege of Vienna had been fended off. This book has the affectionate subtitle: "How the imperial patrimonial lands can be raised above all other states in Europe within a short period by means of a well-tilled economy". There is a baroque double meaning skilfully hidden behind the claim of title of the book: "*wann es nur will*" in German means "whenever" or "as soon as Austria is willing", but also implies the possibility that Austria could rise above everyone else, if only she were willing.

Chronology: Austrian History in the 20th Century

28 July 1914	Outbreak of the First World War.
21 Nov. 1916	Emperor Franz Joseph I. dies and is succeeded by Karl I.
3 March 1918	Peace of Bresk-Litowsk.
30 Oct. 1918	Provisional government under Chancellor Karl Renner, with a constitution for "German-Austria".
3 Nov. 1918	Armistice between Austria-Hungary and the Allied states.
12 Nov. 1918	The provisional National Assembly proclaims the Republic of German-Austria.
16 Feb. 1919	First elections to the National Council.
10 Sept. 1919	Peace Agreement of Saint-Germain en Laye.
1920	Hans Kelsen drafts the new constitution which establishes Austria as a Federal state.
10 June 1920	Coalition government between Christian Socialists and Social Democrats ends; Dr. Ignaz Seipel heads a Christian Socialist government.
15 July 1927	The Palace of Justice is set on fire.
4 March 1933	The National Council is dissolved; Engelbert Dollfuß heads a corporatist (*Ständestaat*) state government.
12–15 Feb. 1934	February Riots, followed by prohibition of the Social Democratic Party.
25 July 1934	Abortive coup by the National Socialists, in the course of which Engelbert Dollfuß is assassinated; Kurt Schuschnigg becomes new Federal Chancellor.
12 Feb. 1938	Talks between Adolf Hitler and Kurt Schuschnigg; National Socialists are included in government.
12 March 1938	German troops march into Austria, one day after Schuschnigg's resignation.
09 Nov. 1938	Pogrom against Jews culminates in the *"Reichskristallnacht"* ("Night of Broken Glass").
01 Sept. 1939	Second World War begins with attack on Poland.
18 Feb. 1942	Churchill declares in a speech "that Austria was the first victim of Nazi aggression".
30 Oct. 1943	Moscow Declaration by the Allied states declares the restoration of Austria as a free, sovereign state as a war goal.
27 April 1945	The provisional state government headed by Karl Renner proclaims the independent Republic of Austria.
08 May 1945	Second World War ends in Europe; Austria is occupied by American, British, French and Soviet troops.
09 July 1945	The Allies divide Austria into zones of occupation.
20 Oct. 1945	Allied powers recognise Renner's government.
25 Nov. 1945	First elections to the National Council in the Second Republic.

30 Nov. 1945	The schilling is re-introduced as Austria's official currency.
20 Dec. 1945	Government of national unity formed under the leadership of Leopold Figl; Karl Renner is elected as Federal President by the Federal Assembly of the Austrian Parliament.
26 July 1946	1st *Verstaatlichtengesetz* (Nationalised Industries Act): The three largest banks as well as enterprises in the iron, steel, chemical and oil sectors are transferred into public ownership, in order to protect them from access by third parties for being former German property. On 26 March 1947 (2nd *Verstaatlichtengesetz* (Nationalised Industries Act)) much of the electricity industry was nationalised.
16 Jan. 1947	First negotiations on the Austrian State Treaty at the deputy foreign ministers conference in London.
25 Feb. 1947	The Austrian national anthem is introduced.
20 Nov. 1947	After the Communist Party (KPÖ) has left the government of national unity, the "grand coalition" between the Socialist Party (SPÖ) and the People's Party (ÖVP) begins.
02 July 1948	Austria joins the Marshall Plan Agreement.
09 April 1949	The Western Allies renounce claims to German property in Austria.
09 Oct. 1949	Less incriminated national socialists are admitted to the general elections for the National Council again; the SPÖ and the ÖVP lose votes to the "Independent Party" (*Wahlpartei der Unabhängigen*).
27 May 1951	In a direct election, Theodor Körner is voted in to become Federal President.
26 April 1952	The reconstructed St. Stephen's Cathedral is reopened.
02 April 1953	Julius Raab (ÖVP) becomes new Federal Chancellor.
16 March 1955	The Federal government declares its intention not to join any military alliance and not to allow for any military bases to be established within Austria's national territory.
11 April 1955	An Austrian government delegation arrives in Moscow for the State Treaty negotiations.
15 May 1955	The Austrian State Treaty is signed.
27 July 1955	Last session of the Allied Council; the State Treaty enters into force.
01 Aug. 1955	Austria's first TV broadcast.
15 Oct. 1955	The Vienna *Burgtheater* is reopened, performing Grillparzer's *"König Ottokars Glück und Ende"* (King Ottocar, His Rise and Fall).
26 Oct. 1955	The National Council enacts the Federal Constitutional Law on Austria's Neutrality.
05 Nov. 1955	The Vienna State Opera is reopened with a performance of Beethoven's *"Fidelio"*.
15 Dec. 1955	Austria joins the United Nations.
05 May 1957	Adolf Schärf (SPÖ) becomes Federal President; he is re-elected in 1963.
11 April 1961	Alfons Gorbach (ÖVP) becomes Federal Chancellor.
04 Jan. 1960	Austria joins EFTA as one of its founder members.
02 April 1964	Josef Klaus (ÖVP) becomes Federal Chancellor.
12 Oct. 1964	The first petition for a referendum supports the request for a reform of public broadcasting.

23 May 1965	Franz Jonas (SPÖ) is elected to become Federal President; he is re-elected in 1971.
19 April 1966	One-party ÖVP government headed by Josef Klaus.
21 April 1970	SPÖ minority government under Bruno Kreisky.
10 Oct. 1971	SPÖ wins an absolute majority in the general election for the National Council.
23 June 1974	Rudolf Kirchschläger is elected to become Federal President; he is re-elected in 1980.
05 Nov. 1978	In a referendum, the Austrian population decides against putting the atomic power plant in Zwentendorf into operation.
24 May 1983	Coalition between SPÖ and FPÖ, headed by Fred Sinowatz.
08 Dez. 1984	The *Hainburger Au* (meadow near Hainburg in Lower Austria) is occupied in order to prevent a Danube power plant from being built.
08 June 1986	Kurt Waldheim is elected as Federal President.
21 Feb. 1987	"Grand coalition", headed by Franz Vranitzky II (SPÖ) until 1997, then headed by Viktor Klima (SPÖ).
17 July 1989	Austria's formal application for EC membership is submitted in Brussels.
24 May 1992	Thomas Klestil is elected Federal President; he is re-elected in 1998.
12 June 1994	In a referendum the Austrian population votes in favour of EU accession (with 66.4% of the popular vote).
01 Jan. 1995	Austria joins the European Union.
13 Oct. 1996	First European parliamentary elections in Austria.
18 July 1997	Austria joins the Schengen Agreement.
01 July – 31 Dec. 1998	Austria holds the EU Council Presidency for the first time.
01 Jan. 2000	Austria holds the chair of the OSCE for one year.
04 Feb. 2000	Coalition between People's Party (ÖVP) and Freedom Party (FPÖ), and later the Alliance for the Future of Austria (BZÖ) under Federal Chancellor Wolfgang Schüssel (ÖVP).
01 Jan. 2002	The euro is introduced as the currency in circulation.
25 April 2004	Heinz Fischer is elected Federal President.
01 Jan. – 30 June 2006	Austria holds the EU Council Presidency.
01 Oct. 2006	The former ÖVP-BZÖ coalition loses its majority in parliament.
08 Jan. 2007	The SPÖ and ÖVP form a "grand coalition" government, with SPÖ leader, Alfred Gusenbauer, becoming chancellor.

Bibliography

Albright, Madeleine K. *The Mighty and the Almighty. Reflections on America, God and World Affairs*, New York 2006.

Androsch, Hannes. *Warum Österreich so ist, wie es ist. Eine Synthese aus Widersprüchen*, Munich/Vienna/Zurich 2003.

Androsch, Hannes. 'Der österreichische Weg – Reminiszenzen und Prospektion', *in: Österreichische Nationalgeschichte nach 1945. Der Spiegel der Erinnerung: Die Sicht von innen,* Vol. I, ed. by Robert Kriechbaumer, Vienna/Cologne/Weimar 1998, p. 559–582.

Androsch, Hannes. *Die politische Ökonomie der österreichischen Währung. Ein Überblick über die österreichische Währungspolitik von 1960 bis 1984 vor dem Hintergrund der internationalen Entwicklung*, Vienna 1985.

Andics, Hellmut. *Der Staat, den keiner wollte*, Vienna 1962.

Bachinger, Karl / Stiefel, Dieter (ed.). *Auf Heller und Cent. Beiträge zur Finanz- und Währungsgeschichte*, Frankfurt/Vienna 2001; especially: Hannes Androsch. 'Österreichische Währungspolitik – vom harten Schilling zum Euro', p. 597ff.

Bahr, Egon. *Der deutsche Weg. Selbstverständlich und normal*, Munich 2003.

Barazon, Ronald. *Kampf dem Kapitalismus*, Salzburg 2006.

Beller, Steven: *A Concise History of Austria*, Cambridge 2006.

Binder, Otto. 'Dr. Rudolf Neumayer und die "Wiener Städtische"', in: *Zwischenwelt. Zeitschrift für Kultur des Exils und des Widerstands*, (Vienna) 21st year, No. 3–4 (March/April 2005), p. 4–16.

Brandstaller, Trautl. 'Drei Gedenkjahre, drei versäumte Gelegenheiten', in: *Das jüdische Echo* Vol. 53 (October 2004), p. 40–44.

Brandt, Willy / Helmut Schmidt. *Deutschland 1976. Zwei Sozialdemokraten im Gespräch*, Gesprächsführung Jürgen Kellermeier, Reinbeck bei Hamburg 1976.

Brittan, Samuel. *Against the Flow. Reflections of an Individualist*, London 2005.

Brzezinski, Zbigniew. *The Great Chessboard. American Primacy and its Geostrategic Imperatives*, New York 1997.

Brzezinski, Zbigniew. *The Choice: Global Domination or Global Leadership*, New York 2004.

Chaloupek, Günther et al. (ed.). *Ökonomie in Theorie und Praxis. Festschrift für Helmut Frisch*, Berlin 2002, see especially: Hannes Androsch: 'Wirtschaftspolitik im globalen Umfeld', p. 1–14.

Clark, Willliam R. *Petrodollar Warfare. Oil, Iraq and the Future of the Dollar*, New York 2005.

Czempiel, Ernst-Otto. *Weltpolitik im Umbruch. Die Pax Americana, der Terrorismus und die Zukunft der internationalen Beziehungen*, Munich 2002.

Dahrendorf, Ralf. 'Europa und die Zukunft des Westens. Ein Gespräch mit Lord Dahrendorf', in: *Blätter für deutsche und internationale Politik* 3/05, p. 288–300.

Defago, Alfred. *Was ist mit Amerika los? Beobachtungen aus einem Land, das anders denkt*, Frauenfeld 2004.

Diamond, Jared. *Guns, Germs and Steel. The Fate of Human Societies*, New York 1997.

Dirninger, Christian (ed.). *Wirtschaftspolitik zwischen Konsens und Konflikt. Einsichten und Einblicke in die Strukturen und Abläufe der Wirtschaftspolitik der Zweiten Republik*, Vienna/Cologne/Weimar 1995.

Dönhoff, Marion Gräfin. *Zivilisiert den Kapitalismus. Grenzen der Freiheit*, Stuttgart 1997.

Economist Intelligence Unit (ed.). *Foresight 2020. Economic, industry and corporate trends*, 2006.

Ehalt, Hubert Christian (ed.). 'Schlaraffenland? Europa neu denken. Auf der Suche nach einer neuen Identität für den alten Kontinent', in: *Bibliothek urbaner Kultur*, Vol. I, Weitra o.J.

Eizenstat, Stuart E. *Imperfect Justice. Looted Assets, Slave Labor, and the Unfinished Business of World War II*, New York 2003.

Fukuyama, Francis. *The End of the History and the Last Man*, New York 1992.

Fukuyama, Francis. *After the Neocons. Where the Right went Wrong: America at the Crossroads*, London 2006.

Galbraith, John Kenneth. *The Affluent Society*, London 1970.

Garton Ash, Timothy. *Free World. Why a crisis in the West Reveals the Opportunity of our time*, London 2004.

Heinberg, Richard. *The Party's Over. Oil, War and the Fate of Industrial Societies*, New York 2003.

Hobsbawm, Eric J. *The Age of Empire 1875–1914*, London 1987.

Hobsbawm, Eric J. *Age of Extremes. The Short Twentieth Century 1914–1991*, London 1994.

Hörnigk, Friedrich Wilhelm von. *Österreich über alles, wann es nur will. Wie mittels einer wohlbestellten Landesökonomie die kaiserlichen Erblande in kurzem über alle anderen Staaten Europas zu erheben sind*, Vienna 1684.

Huemer, Peter. *Sektionschef Dr. Robert Hecht und die Entstehung der ständisch-autoritären Verfassung in Österreich*, Vol. 1–2, Wien (Univ. Diss.) 1968.

Hutton, Will. *The World we're in*, London 2002.

Hutton, Will. *The Writing on the Wall. Why We Must Embrace China as a Partner of Face It as an Enemy*, New York 2006.

James, Harold. *Europe reborn. A history 1914–2000* (Longman) 2003

Jay, Peter. *The Wealth of Man*, London 2000.

Jochmann, Rosa. *Ein Kampf der nie zu Ende geht. Reden und Aufsätze*, ed. by Hans Waschek, Vienna 1994.

Judt, Tony. *Postwar. A History of Europe since 1945*, London 2005.

Kagan, Robert. *Of Paradise and Power*, New York 2003.

Keynes, John M. *The Economic Consequences of the Peace*, London 1920.

Kissinger, Henry A. *Does America need a Foreign Policy? Toward a Diplomacy for the Twenty-First Century*, New York 2001.

Kissinger, Henry A. 'Renewing the Atlantic Partnership', in: *Council on Foreign Relations* 2004.

Klare, Michael T. *Resource Wars. The New Landscape of Global Conflict*, New York 2001.

Kleveman, Lutz. *The Great Game. Blood and Oil in Central Asia*, New York 2003.

Kopeinig, Margaretha. *Jean-Claude Juncker. Der Europäer*, Wien 2004.

Koren, Stephan. *Wirtschaftsforscher und Wirtschaftspolitiker in Österreich*, ed. by Werner Clement und Karl Socher, Wien 1989.

Krugman, Paul. *The Great Unravelling. From Boom to Bust in Three Scandalous Years*, London 2003.

Krugman, Paul. *The Return of Depression Economics*, New York 1999.

Kupchan, Charles. *The End of the American Era*, New York 2002.

Lübbe, Hermann. *Abschied vom Superstaat. Vereinigte Staaten von Europa wird es nicht geben*, Berlin 1994.

Mazower, Mark. *Dark Continent: Europe's Twentieth Century*, London 1998.

Meadows, Dennis. *The Limits to Growth. A Report for the Club of Rome's Project on the Predicament of Mankind*, London 1972.

Mitterauer, Michael. *Warum Europa? Mittelalterliche Grundlagen eines Sonderwegs*, Munich 1993.

Neugebauer, Wolfgang / Peter Schwarz: *Der Wille zum aufrechten Gang. Offenlegung der Rolle des BSA bei der gesellschaftlichen Reintegration ehemaliger Nationalsozialisten*, Vienna 2005.

Ney, Joseph S. *The Paradox of American Power. Why the world's only superpower can't go it alone*, New York 2002.

Nölling, Wilhelm et al. (ed.): *Währungsunion und Weltwirtschaft. Festschrift für Wilhelm Hankel*, Stuttgart 1999, see especially: Hannes Androsch. 'Aspekte des Geld- und Währungswesens als ökonomisches Rüstzeug und wirtschaftspolitisches Präzisionsinstrument', p. 227–238.

Pelinka, Anton / Erika Weinzierl (ed.). *Das große Tabu. Österreichs Umgang mit seiner Vergangenheit*, Vienna 1997.

Portisch, Hugo. *Österreich II*, Vol. 1–4, Munich 1993.
Prestowitz, Clyde V. *Three Billion New Capitalists: The Great Shift of Wealth and Power to the East*, New York 2005.
Rifkin, Jeremy. *The European Dream*, New York 2004.
Schärf, Adolf. *Österreichs Erneuerung 1945–1955. Das erste Jahrzehnt der Zweiten Republik*, Vienna 1955.
Scheuch, Manfred. *Österreich im 20. Jahrhundert*, Vienna 2000.
Scheuch, Manfred. *Der Weg zum Heldenplatz. Eine Geschichte der österreichischen Diktatur 1933–1938*, Munich/Vienna/Zurich 2005.
Schmidt, Helmut. *Die Selbstbehauptung Europas. Perspektiven für das 21. Jahrhundert*, Stuttgart/Munich 2000.
Schulze, Hagen. *Staat und Nation in der Europäischen Geschichte*, Munich 1994.
Seidel, Hans. 'Austro-Keynesianismus – revisited', in: F. Weber and Th. Venus (ed.). *Austro-Keynesianismus in Theorie und Praxis*, Vienna 1993.
Seidel, Hans. *Österreichs Wirtschaft und Wirtschaftspolitik nach dem Zweiten Weltkrieg*, Vienna 2005.
Seitz, Konrad. *Wettlauf ins 21. Jahrhundert. Die Zukunft Europas zwischen Amerika und Asien*, Berlin 1998.
Seitz, Konrad. 'China im 21. Jahrhundert', in: *Alfred Herrhausen Gesellschaft für internationalen Dialog*, Frankfurt am Main 3/2000.
Soros, George. *Die offene Gesellschaft. Für eine Reform des Globalen Kapitalismus*, Berlin 2001.
Steinbach, Günther. *Schicksalstage Europas. 10 Ereignisse, die den Kontinent prägten*, Vienna 2002.
Steinbach, Günther. *Europas unruhiges Herz. Die 10 wichtigsten Stationen der deutschen Geschichte*, Vienna 2003.
Steinbach, Günther. *Kanzler, Krisen, Katastrophen. Die Erste Republik*, Vienna 2006.
Stiglitz, Joseph. *Globalization and Its Discontents*, New York 2002.
Stourzh, Gerald. *Um Einheit und Freiheit. Staatsvertrag, Neutralität und das Ende der Ost-West-Besetzung*

Österreichs 1945–1955 (Studien zu Politik und Verwaltung, Vol. 62), Vienna/Cologne/Graz 1998.

Stürmer, Michael. *Die Kunst des Gleichgewichts. Europa in einer Welt ohne Mitte*, Berlin/Munich 2001.

Stürmer, Michael. *Welt ohne Weltordnung. Wer wird die Erde erben?* Hamburg 2006.

Tettamanti, Tito. *Die sieben Sünden des Kapitals. Erfahrungen eines Unternehmers*, Zurich 2003.

Triffin, Robert. *Gold and the Dollar Crisis: The Future of Convertibility*, Yale University Press 1961.

Weissensteiner, Friedrich. *Der ungeliebte Staat. Österreich zwischen 1918 und 1938*, Vienna 1990.

Weizsäcker, Ernst Ulrich von. *Limits to Privatization. How to avoid too much of a good thing. A Report to the Club of Rome*, London 2005.

Yergin, Daniel. *Prize: The Epic Quest for Oil, Money and Power*, New York 1992.

About the Author

Dr. Hannes Androsch, born in 1938; degree from the *Hochschule für Welthandel* (University of International Trade) in Vienna; first became a certified auditor and tax consultant; from 1964 to 1983 member of the *Bezirksvorstand* (District Board), and from 1984 to 1995 Deputy Chairman of the Social Democratic Party's (SPÖ's) district branch in Floridsdorf (21st district of Vienna); from 1967 to 1981 Member of Parliament (National Council), and from 1974 to 1981 Deputy Party Chairman of the Social Democratic Party.

In 1970, Dr. Bruno Kreisky appointed Dr. Hannes Androsch as Federal Minister for Finance, and in 1976 made him Vice-Chancellor.

After Dr. Hannes Androsch left politics in 1981, he was General Director of Creditanstalt (a large Austrian bank) until 1988. He is still active as an industrialist. Amongst others, Dr. Androsch is Chairman of the University Council of the Leoben University of Mining and Metallurgy, has set up a foundation at the Austrian Academy of Sciences, and holds numerous honorary offices. He also contributed significantly to the realisation of the exhibition "The New Austria" on the Austrian State Treaty in the Austrian Gallery Belvedere in Vienna.

Dr. Androsch has written numerous articles and commentaries on business and politics and is also author and co-editor of several books, the latest of which is *Warum Österreich so ist, wie es ist. Eine Synthese aus Widersprüchen* (Why Austria is What It Is. A Synthesis of Contradictions).

www.androsch.com